THE GEOPOLITICS
OF EMOTION

DOMINIQUE MOÏSI

•

THE GEOPOLITICS
OF EMOTION

•

How Cultures of Fear, Humiliation,
and Hope Are Reshaping the World

DOUBLEDAY

New York   London   Toronto   Sydney   Auckland

ŒD

DOUBLEDAY

Copyright © 2009 by Dominique Moïsi

All Rights Reserved

Published in the United States by Doubleday,
a division of Random House, Inc., New York.
www.doubleday.com

DOUBLEDAY and the DD colophon are registered
trademarks of Random House, Inc.

Book design by Michael Collica

Library of Congress Cataloging-in-Publication Data

Moïsi, Dominique.
The geopolitics of emotion : how cultures of fear,
humiliation, and hope are reshaping the world /
Dominique Moïsi. — 1st ed.
p.   cm.
Includes bibliographical references and index.
1. Globalization—Psychological aspects.
2. Cultural relations—Psychological aspects.
3. Geopolitics—Psychological aspects. I. Title.
JZ1318.M64 2009
303.48'2—dc22
2008044798

ISBN 978-0-385-52376-9

PRINTED IN THE UNITED STATES OF AMERICA

2 4 6 8 10 9 7 5 3 1

First Edition

To the memory of my father, Jules Moïsi,

number 159721 in Auschwitz,

who survived extreme fear and humiliation to teach me hope

CONTENTS

Preface to the American Edition

On November 4, 2008, like millions of people the world over, I watched the victory celebration for the election of President Barack Obama in Chicago's Grant Park. It was a night of many images laden with emotion. For me, the most powerful symbol of that remarkable night was the tears of joy streaming down the face of the Reverend Jesse Jackson. Those tears reminded me of other images from almost twenty years before—images like that of the great Russian composer Mstislav Rostropovitch, exiled from his homeland, now playing his cello before celebrating crowds in front of the crumbling Berlin Wall. They were tears of triumph and reconciliation, tears of harmony with the world, tears whose joyous message was that men and women can change history for the best when moved by emotions—the *right* emotions.

Less than a month later, in Mumbai—the city that is a symbol of hope of India—the "wrong emotions" were at work, as humiliation turned into terrorist violence. "Why are you doing this to us?" a man who had been taken hostage and was about to be executed called out to the gunmen. "We haven't done anything to you."

"Remember Babri Masjid?" one of the gunmen shouted in reply. He was referring to a sixteenth-century mosque built by

India's first Mughal Muslim emperor and destroyed by Hindu radicals in 1962. "Remember Godhra?" a second attacker asked. He was referring to the town in the Indian state of Gujarat, where religious rioting that evolved into an anti-Muslim pogrom began in 2002. The incident is further testimony, if any is needed, to the enduring power of symbols—in this case, symbols of humiliation—to evoke emotions and thereby control human behavior, even after a lapse of centuries.

The very title of this book, *The Geopolitics of Emotion*, will strike many critics as a sheer provocation, if not an oxymoron. After all, isn't geopolitics about rationality, about objective data such as frontiers, economic resources, military might, and the cold political calculus of interest? By contrast, emotions are essentially subjective, if not purely irrational. To mix emotions and geopolitics can only be a futile, perhaps dangerous exercise, leading ultimately to the abyss of unreason epitomized by the pagan masses at Nuremburg during Germany's descent into barbarity under Hitler.

Perhaps so. And yet this book is based on a dual conviction. First: One cannot fully understand the world in which we live without trying to integrate and understand its emotions. And second, emotions are like cholesterol, both good and bad. The problem is to find the right balance between them.

In November 2008, at least for a time, hope prevailed over fear. The wall of racial prejudice fell as surely as the wall of oppression had fallen in Berlin twenty years earlier. Obviously there were objective, rational reasons for Obama's victory. In normal political terms, it was a rejection of the policies of the previous administration during a time of prolonged warfare and deep economic crisis. Yet the emotional dimension of this election and the sense of pride it created in many Americans must not be underestimated.

In the same vein, it is impossible to understand the Russian military adventures in the Caucasus in the summer of 2008 without considering their emotional meaning. The message being sent by the Moscow regime of Putin and Medvedev, not only to the Georgians but to the people of the world, was quite clear: "Imperial Russia is back! After 1989, you dared to condescend to us. Those days are over. We are ready to transcend our post-Soviet humiliation, erecting our new hope on the foundation of your fear."

During that same summer of 2008, another regime sought to transcend past humiliation on the global stage, not through military adventurism but through international sport. By hosting the Olympic Games, China symbolically—and emotionally—reclaimed its historic centrality and its international legitimacy. Through the majesty of the opening ceremony, the architectural beauty of the stadium, and the many medals won by its athletes, China passed the test of entrance into modernity, attaining a new pinnacle of hope fueled by soaring economic growth.

Yet even as China grasps for hope, the Arab world remains mired in tragedy and the negative emotion of humiliation. Not all Arabs—not even a majority—subscribe to the irrational and hateful doctrines of violent jihad against the West. But even many Arab moderates reject notions of peaceful change and active citizenship, assuming that all political leaders are dishonest and corrupt. The attitude may be understandable, but it reflects and reinforces the feeling of despair that limits progress throughout the Arab world.

Fear against hope, hope against humiliation, humiliation leading to sheer irrationality and even, sometimes, to violence—one cannot comprehend the world in which we live without examining the emotions that help to shape it.

As I write these lines in the aftermath of Barack Obama's election, the financial and economic crisis is deepening and widening throughout the world, affecting even Asia, the continent that until recently had been the primary driver of global economic growth. Which will prevail on the planetary stage—the spirit of hope carried by Obama's victory, or the spirit of fear driven by economic collapse? It is, of course, impossible to predict. Much will depend upon the ability of the new American president to transform words into deeds, and to restore and rehabilitate politics in the eyes of his nation's citizens. But much also depends on the quality of Chinese leadership, which is now faced with its greatest challenge in decades. For the first time in recent memory, the future of the planet will no longer be determined only by decisions taken by the democratic West. We may soon discover whether centralized, nondemocratic regimes such as

China's may actually be better equipped to respond to economic crises than democratic countries such as the United States.

This book has its own history, a bit reminiscent of a set of traditional Russian nesting dolls. It began with my Project Syndicate column of March 2006, titled "The Emotional Clash of Civilizations." My former professor and now colleague at Harvard University, Stanley Hoffmann, encouraged me to develop it into a short essay, which was then published in the American journal *Foreign Affairs* in January 2007. This article, titled "The Clash of Emotions," initiated a lively debate, and I was invited to present and defend my thesis widely in the American media, including an appearance on the popular National Public Radio program *To the Point*. One of my listeners, Charlie Conrad, a top executive at Random House, asked me to transform my *Foreign Affairs* essay into a book. This is how *The Geopolitics of Emotion* came to life.

Of course, by contrast to the essay on which it was based, the book is far more fully developed and therefore more nuanced in its presentation. Furthermore, the world has been radically transformed in the last two years. If there is as much humiliation as before, hope and fear both seem to have grown exponentially and in a very parallel manner. Yet the central thesis of the book has not changed. After all, emotions remain crucial to understanding the nature and evolution of the world, and it seems likely that this will be the case as long as the human species survives.

Dominique Moïsi
Paris
November 24, 2008

THE GEOPOLITICS
OF EMOTION

Introduction

THE CLASH OF EMOTIONS

Globalization is great, but it is not for us. We are not Asians or Westerners. We cannot make it; we will not make it."

It was the summer of 2000. I had been invited to chair an international conference on globalization at the University of Al Akhawayn, a school of management set up jointly by the kings of Morocco and Saudi Arabia in the Atlas Mountains city of Ifrane, sixty kilometers west of Fez. English was the teaching language of the school, and the students would not have looked out of place at a university in California or Ohio. The veil was forbidden; young men and young women were walking hand in hand, when they were not casually lying next to each other on the immaculate grass, whose shining green stood out from the arid environment surrounding the campus.

Curious about the presence of a Frenchman at this international gathering, the students invited me to join them one night. They spoke to me in French, a language still more familiar to them than English. They were fascinated by globalization, but they wanted to talk to me about their fundamental doubts about themselves and their future. I was struck by the lack of self-confidence expressed in the words of one student: "Globalization is not for us." These young people belonged to the elite of Morocco; they were the children of the middle class that many hoped would make a fundamental difference in the future of their country. What was the cause of their deep pessimism about their ability to master the future?

Several possible explanations occurred to me. Perhaps they were doubtful about the political prospects of their government. (The students expressed praise for the new king, who had just ascended to the throne, but the skeptical expressions on their faces belied their words.) Or perhaps their lack of confidence was linked to their country's geographical position—so close to Europe but on the "wrong side" of the Mediterranean—or to their cultural and religious heritage.

Whatever the reason, their message to me was clear: If they were to succeed in the world of globalization, it would be one by one, as solitary individuals on the world stage rather than as representatives of their homeland, and it probably would not happen in Morocco.

At an international gathering in Germany a few years later I met a bright young Moroccan professor teaching in a North American university. Coming from a very poor rural background in southern Morocco, he had been selected for a king's scholarship by Hassan II to study abroad, but he had never received the grant because of the climate of corruption dominating the country. Some bureaucrat had channeled the money to someone else, most probably a well-connected student with access to the country's elite. Through a circuitous route, he had finally and miraculously "made it," but he had done so clearly on his own. He was an outsider to his own country, and he had no intention of returning to it.

In the winter of 2006 I visited India for the first time. Arriving in Mumbai, one of the symbols of India's economic miracle, I was fascinated by what I saw. On my journey from the airport to the center of the city, I was quickly reminded that India has the largest underclass in the world: Amid the incessant, noisy traffic, the poor and homeless lived by the side of the road. Yet I was impressed by the sheer energy of the city; Mumbai seemed to emanate hope.

Suketu Mehta, an Indian writer and journalist now based in New York, explains the spirit I sensed on that visit. Mumbai, he says, is a place "where your caste doesn't matter, where a woman can dine alone at a restaurant without harassment, and where you can marry the person of your choice. For the young person in an Indian village, the call of Mumbai isn't just about money. It's also about freedom." I was struck by this tremendous sense of optimism. The very poor keep streaming into Mumbai motivated by the conviction that even if they are unable to improve their own lives, their children or their grandchildren will have a better chance.

The contrast between the affluent young people of Morocco and the poor of Mumbai is striking. While the former perceive globalization as a challenge already lost, the latter, against all odds, see it as an opportunity.

And now a third vignette from yet another city. On July 7, 2007, I was walking the streets of London. It was exactly a year after the bombings that had racked the city in 2006. I felt that the memory of these events was very much on everybody's mind. Late for a meeting, I boarded a train in the tube (London's underground train system) and found that the tension was palpable. When and where would the next terrorist attack take place? The few travelers eyed one another suspiciously. At one tube station, a young woman with a veil nearly covering her face and carrying a heavy bag while intoning what sounded like a prayer came into the car and sat in front of me. I suddenly felt my last hour had come. It was clear to me that she was going to blow herself up. I felt terror in my spine; I could barely breathe. At the next station I rushed out of the train. I wasn't the only one to do so, for fear pervaded most other passengers as well.

The young woman remained nearly alone in the carriage, her solitude reflecting our combination of fear and prejudice. Her veil not only protected her "virtue" but had also isolated her by creating in our eyes something like a halo of terror that surrounded her like a moving minefield.

Here I was in the financial capital of the world, a bustling, affluent city that was also—at least that day—dominated by fear.

Humiliation in Ifrane, hope in Mumbai, fear in London. Do these three vignettes and the three differing moods they contained signify anything beyond themselves? Do they represent underlying cultural tendencies characteristic of particular regions and populations today? If so, how might these varying emotions influence the political, social, and cultural conflicts that roil our world? These are questions I have been wrestling with for the past several years.

There was a time when students of international affairs tacitly discounted the importance of emotions. Global politics was the reserved field of a special caste of professionals, mostly European aristocrats, who looked on world politics as a game of chess. States and governments were supposed to act rationally. Emotions were to be kept at bay, for they introduced additional irrationality into a world that was already in a natural state of disorder. Emotions therefore were contained and organized by international agreements designed to provide structure in an unruly world. Thus the Treaty of Westphalia in 1648, product of history's first great international congress, ended the Thirty Years War and established a European settlement that would hold passions, such as religious fervor, in check.

Of course emotions aren't easily contained. They burst out again—with a vengeance—with the French Revolution in 1789 but then were repressed again, from the Congress of Vienna in 1815, which concluded the end of the Napoleonic adventure, until the revolutions of 1848.

Between the Russian Revolution in 1917 and the fall of the Berlin Wall in 1989, ideologies replaced national passions. One might even call the twentieth century the era of ideology. It was the passing of that era that led historian Francis Fukuyama to conclude—prematurely, of course—that history itself had come to an end. It was an understandable mistake. After all, for several generations, history had been driven by ideological conflict; now that one side of the major conflict of that era had collapsed, wasn't it natural to assume that the to-and-fro struggle that constitutes history might itself come to an end?

It was not to be, of course. Today, as we shall see, quests for identity by peoples uncertain of who they are, their place in the world, and their prospects for a meaningful future have replaced ideology as the motor of history, with the consequence that emotions matter more than ever in a world where media are playing the role of a sounding board and a magnifying glass.

In a larger sense, however, emotions—whether religious,

national, ideological, or even purely personal—have of course always mattered. Throughout the nineteenth and twentieth centuries, emotions were at the forefront of politics. Even philosopher Immanuel Kant in Königsberg was moved to stop working on the day of the battle of Valmy in 1792, when the armies of the French Revolution defeated the allied coalition fighting to defend the ancien régime, one of just two events supposed to have disrupted Kant's famously rigid personal self-discipline. (The other, legend has it, was the publication of Rousseau's *Du contrat social* in 1762.) The totalitarian movements of the twentieth century were *passionately* ideological. Without our recognizing the crucial influence of emotions, which seem to control us much more than we control them, it is simply impossible to understand the course of history.

In this book, I have chosen to focus on three primary emotions: fear, hope, and humiliation. But why these three? Why not anger, despair, hatred, resentment, rage, love, honor, solidarity . . . ? The reason I have chosen these three emotions is that they are closely linked with the the the notion of *confidence*, which is the defining factor in how nations and people address the challenges they face as well as how they relate to one another.

Fear is the absence of confidence. If your life is dominated by fear, you are apprehensive about the present and expect the future to become ever more dangerous. Hope, by contrast, is an expression of confidence; it is based on the conviction that today is better than yesterday and that tomorrow will be better than today. And humiliation is the injured confidence of those who have lost hope in the future; your lack of hope is the fault of others, who have treated you badly in the past. When the contrast between your idealized and glorious past and your frustrating present is too great, humiliation prevails.

If one wanted to summarize these three emotions with three formulas, one would say that hope is "I want to do it, I can do it, and I will do it"; humiliation is "I can never do it" and may lead to "I might try as well to destroy you since I cannot join you"; and fear is "Oh, my God, the world has become such a dangerous place; how can I be protected from it?"

These three emotions express the level of trust you have in yourself. Confidence is as vital for nations and civilizations as for individuals, because confidence allows you to project yourself into the future, to fulfill your capabilities, and even to transcend them. Confidence (distinguished from hubris) is one of the most important components of the world's health.

How, one might ask, is a quality as abstract as "confidence" to be measured on a national level? There are several ways. Confidence may be measured in an objective as well as a subjective manner. Some of its indicators may seem, at first glance, somewhat trivial. For example, in today's world, where sports relayed by media have become the equivalent of a secular religion, triumph on the playing field may even, if briefly, bolster the morale of a population and have a measurable impact on national confidence. Consider for a moment the impact of the U.S. hockey team's "Miracle on Ice" victory over the Soviet Union in the 1980 Olympics or the more recent European examples of France's victory in the 1998 Mundial and Spain's 2008 triumph in the 2008 Euro championship. When your team wins on the global stage, you feel "on top of the world," united in a collective manner with the national team whose triumph you share.

National confidence may be expressed in architecture, art, or music. Think of seventeenth-century Dutch painting, the art of a golden age reflecting the pride in what had been achieved economically, socially, and politically by the mercantile middle class of the Netherlands. Think of the music of Purcell, which celebrates the glory of postrevolutionary England.

In a more objective way, confidence can be mapped by so-called confidence indicators, which measure scientifically the level of trust of a population in its own future, most concretely in its spending patterns. Confidence is also expressed by levels of investment. For example, the current resurgence of national confidence in the former Soviet Union was indicated by the way Russians had resumed investing their money in their own country.

Birthrates are a more complex indicator. Economic and social progress often leads to a growing individualism, which may lead in turn to a reduction of birthrates, accompanied by rising prosperity. But economic and social despair may also produce a decline in the birthrate, reflecting not prosperity but hopelessness.

In geopolitics, confidence may be expressed by agreements

between states. From that standpoint, confidence-building measures established between China and India in the early 1990s reflect the growing hopefulness of the two Asian giants.

Of course emotions, including humiliation, hope, and fear, are often much more thoroughly intertwined than my vignettes illustrate. Fear is never far from hope, and you would not have to dig very deep to find humiliation lurking behind fear or even hope.

This book reflects the personal journey of a "passionately moderate" man who has dedicated his life to the study of international relations. I've become convinced that simplified views of the world—whether overly positive, like Fukuyama's celebration of "democracy's triumph," or overly negative, like Samuel Huntington's "clash of civilizations"—are simply dangerous. For that reason, this book offers no all-encompassing theory of the world. Instead it seeks to provide a corrective to the simplified views that tend to dominate most discourse. It is about the mix of emotions and the shades of gray most truly characteristic of our world.

I am of course not alone in my emphasis on the importance of emotions. From Plato to Hobbes, from Kant to Hegel, philosophers have always emphasized the role and influence of the classical concept of passion as opposed to the Marxist notion of class interest, in which people interact as a function of their social and economic status. However, this is not a book about the history of emotions. It is an essay on globalization and the necessity to confront emotions to understand our changing world, an attempt, one might say, to map globalization in an emotional way.

In this search, I am indebted to my intellectual mentors, Stanley Hoffmann at Harvard and Pierre Hassner in Paris, who have emphasized in their work the influence of emotions on geopolitics. They both were my professors before I became their colleague and friend, and like me, they are both disciples of Raymond Aron. In his various essays, Pierre Hassner has opened my eyes to the complexities of the world and the dangers of simplification, while Stanley Hoffmann, the most open and generous teacher I have ever met, supported me in my deep conviction that it was realistic to be moral.

My approach in this work is nevertheless different from theirs. It is both much more impressionistic and global, making deliberate use of personal anecdotes and artistic and cultural references. It is a very personal undertaking, in which I have tried to express my own thoughts and emotions even as I explore the impact of human emotions in general on the great events unfolding in the world around us. My hope is that the observations I offer here will resonate with the reader, who in turn will develop from them some deeper insights into the trends shaping our world and the most effective ways we can respond.

Chapter One

GLOBALIZATION, IDENTITY, AND EMOTIONS

In an age of globalization, emotions have become indispensable to grasp the complexity of the world we live in. Magnified by media, they both reflect and react to globalization and in turn influence geopolitics. Globalization may have made the world "flat," to cite journalist Thomas Friedman's famous metaphor, but it has also made the world more passionate than ever.

In a moment, we shall examine the reasons that this is true. But first we need to clarify the nature of globalization itself, since many people misunderstand it. In his book *The Lexus and the Olive Tree*, Friedman defines globalization as the international system that replaced that of the Cold War. Unlike the Cold War system, globalization is not static but a dynamic ongoing process, involving the inexorable integration of markets, nation-states, and technologies to a degree never before witnessed, in a way that is enabling individuals, corporations, and countries to reach around the world farther, faster, deeper, and cheaper than ever before. This same process is also producing a powerful backlash from those brutalized or left behind by the new system.

For many people, especially critics, globalization is identical with Americanization. The spread of American influence—political, economic, and cultural—dates back at least to the Second World War, but it gained new strength after the end

of the Soviet empire in 1991, which left the United States as
the world's only superpower. Thus the growing unification of
the world's economies and cultures means in effect a unification on American terms. As a result, today's antiglobalization
protest movements, which are now mounting with the deepening of the current financial and economic crisis, combine
anti-American sentiments with anticapitalist critiques in their
struggle for equality, fair trade, and sustainable development.

But when we look closer, we see that the equation of globalization with Americanization is too simplistic. The reality is that
while the cultural influence of the United States throughout
the world is all-pervasive and unprecedented, economically the
West is being overtaken by Asia. The current phase of globalization reflects the coming-of-age of the Asian continent, resulting
in the relay of economic power from an American-dominated
West to China and India.

Globalization can thus be seen as the combination of two
disparate phenomena, which may be seen as either contradictory or complementary. On the one hand, we witness the impact of the cultural Americanization of the world. The French
economist Daniel Cohen believes that the gradual reduction of
birthrates in the Southern Hemisphere is the direct result of
the popularity of American television series, families with two
children having become a universal ideal. On the other hand,
the economic rise of Asia is bringing about the end of the monopoly of the Western model. Western predominance in the
world, which began with the establishment of the Raj in India
in the mid-eighteenth century and the decline of China in the
early nineteenth and culminated in the early part of the twentieth century, seems to be coming to an end. This comes as no
surprise to historians of empire, who have long known that the
rise and fall of empires follow a cyclical pattern.

This leads to a situation of asymmetric multipolarity: The
key actors on the world stage not only are unequal in terms of
power and influence but also differ dramatically in their views
of the world. While America and Europe still approach world affairs in a normative manner on the basis of a belief in universal
values, China and India and now also post-Communist Russia
appear far less interested in what the world should become than

in their own positions of power within it. (Thus, for example, Russia's oil and gas wealth is not supposed to contribute to the improvement of life on the planet but to restore the strength and legitimacy of Russia in the international system.)

Such a pragmatic approach is evident in China's view of Singapore. That city-state, with its fusion of Confucian values and eighteenth-century-style enlightened despotism, has played a major role in the evolution of modern China. When, in February 1978, China's new leader, Deng Xiaoping, stopped in Singapore on a diplomatic visit, he did not recognize the "mosquito dump" he remembered from the 1920s. Barely a decade after achieving its independence in 1965, Singapore was already a prosperous city that had embraced capitalism under the firm but enlightened guidance of Lee Kuan Yew. Once liberated from a narrow socialist economic vision, Lee Kuan Yew argued to Deng Xiaoping, the Communist heirs of the mandarins of the Middle Empire should be able to do even better economically than the descendants of poor Chinese peasants from the south. And indeed this has been the broader vision that Deng and the rest of China's leaders have followed.

For China, this pragmatic approach has paid off. The country's remarkable economic progress has been achieved without democracy, even without the rule of law.

In the rest of the world, meanwhile, democracy has been dangerously devalued through the inflationary use of the word by the Bush administration in its attempt to justify the United States' geopolitical ambitions. The contrast between the democratic ideal and the reality of democratic practices in too many Western and non-Western countries may explain in part the relay of power from America to Asia that I have described.

If democracies are losing faith in democratic models, and if autocratic regimes are supported in their antidemocratic practices by their combination of high economic growth and political stability, it is the Western world that suffers most from this evolution. Less than twenty years ago, in the immediate aftermath of the fall of the Berlin Wall, the West enjoyed a sense of supremacy because of its democratic values that more than compensated for the fact that countries like the newly united Germany were not doing well economically. But today the democratic essence of the West is no longer seen as compensating for its lack of economic performance. Maybe emotions have returned to the forefront of the international scene in part because the West can no longer rely on either its values or its fading economic supremacy and therefore reacts to global changes with a certain bitterness and a desire to protect its precious open world against hostile forces.

But the primary reason that today's globalizing world is the ideal fertile ground for the blossoming or even the explosion of emotions is that globalization causes insecurity and raises the question of identity. In the Cold War period there was never any reason to ask, "Who are we?" The answer was plainly visible on every map that depicted the two adversarial systems dividing the globe between them. But in an ever-changing world without borders, the question is intensely relevant. Identity is strongly linked with confidence, and in turn confidence, or the lack thereof, is expressed in emotions—in particular, those of fear, hope, and humiliation.

Economically, globalization can be defined simply as the integration of economic activities across borders through markets. The driving forces of globalization, masterfully analyzed by Martin Wolf, are technological and policy changes that reduce the costs of transport and communications and encourage greater reliance on market forces. But this free flow of goods in economic terms also implies in political terms the free flow of emotions, including both positive emotions (ambition, curiosity, yearning for self-expression) and evil ones, including the angry passions that lead to hatred between nations, religions, and ethnic groups. Thus terrorism has become the dark, tragic face of globalization.

I don't mean to imply that contemporary terrorism is a direct result of globalization. Terrorists have always crossed borders in pursuit of their goals (notably in nineteenth-century Europe), and the terrorism of al Qaeda has its origins in the specific political situation of the Middle East, which predates and is quite distinct from globalization. But what is new is the impact of the communications and transportation revolutions on the strategy and tactics of the terrorists, with the media revolution (including the Internet) providing new and powerful sounding boards for the terrorist message. New technologies have created a world where, to adapt the words of Churchill, "Never have so few been able to do so much harm to so many."

In a world where the West no longer has a monopoly on the media, events and conflicts can be reported from a variety of angles. The invasion of Lebanon by Israel in the summer of 2006, for instance, appeared as two entirely different wars depending on whether one viewed the coverage on Al Jazeera or on CBS news. In today's world, everyone has access not only to continuing information but also to unfolding emotions. Now that American television series reach all corners of the world and have nearly become universal frames of reference, the poor know how the rich live, and vice versa. As a result, it has become increasingly difficult for the rich to ignore the world's poor, whose anger they witness on the evening news. Many poor people risk their lives by crossing seas and climbing barriers to enter the world of the rich; others who stay at home develop an abiding hatred for the affluent who deliberately ignore their fate.

After 9/11, the brother of one of the al Qaeda terrorists, imprisoned by the American authorities before he could join the nineteen other conspirators, was interviewed on French television. He described his brother as a young man who "wanted to succeed at the top of Wall Street or destroy to ashes the world that would not make a place for him." Such a statement would be impossible if Wall Street and the Islamic Middle East still occupied separate worlds, as they once did.

In a transparent world the poor are no longer ignorant of the world of the rich, and the rich have lost the privilege of denial. They may choose to ignore the tragedies of the developing world, but it is a choice they must make consciously and, increasingly, at their own peril. "Not to act is to act," the theologian Dietrich Bonhoeffer used to say. Today not to intervene to alleviate the sufferings of the world is a form of intervention.

Thus globalization has created a process of universal benchmarking that makes the West more vulnerable. This is true even by comparison with the era of the Cold War, with its ever-present threat of nuclear annihilation, a threat that was both less diffused and more visible and therefore, in retrospect, more emotionally manageable, even "reassuring." When West and East confronted each other across a metaphorical wall (made real, of course, in Berlin), the enemy was singular, easy to identify, and capable of being analyzed, deterred, and negotiated with. Now all that has changed, and the enemy comes not only from another cultural and religious domain but seemingly from another era, one with premodern historical and political references.

The privatization of violence through terrorism; the fact that more conflicts are internal and not external (civil wars rather than international conflicts); the invisible nature of the terrorist threats; and the multiplication of nonpolitical threats such as global pandemics and climate change: All these factors have contributed to a sense of insecurity, vulnerability, and fear. Today in the West we live with an apprehension that can be formulated in one question: What kind of world will our children inherit? Will the combination of spectacular demographic trends—leading, according to projections, to a world of nine billion people by 2050—and worsening shortages of energy, water, and other commodities produce extreme planetary tensions and even wars of sheer survival?

If the twentieth century was both "the American century" and "the century of ideology," I think there is strong evidence that the twenty-first century will be "the Asian century" and "the century of identity." The parallel shifts from ideology to identity and from West to East mean that emotions have become more important than ever in the way we see the world.

In the ideological atmosphere of the twentieth century, the world was defined by conflicting political models: socialism, fascism, and capitalism. In today's world, ideology has been replaced by the struggle for identity. In the age of globalization, when everything and everybody are connected, it is important to assert one's individuality: "I am unique, I am different, and, if necessary, I am willing to fight until you recognize my existence." A Slovak is not a Czech, and a citizen of Montenegro is not a Serb. In a world dominated by identity, we are defined less by our political beliefs and ideas than by the perception of our essence, by the confidence we gain from our achievements and the respect we receive from others or by the lack thereof.

In this perception of our essence, emotions come into play,

linked to the way we look at others as much as to the way others look at us. Emotions are at the same time the image in the mirror and the eye of the person who beholds that image. Emotions are reciprocal, as powerfully illustrated, for instance, by the modern well-educated Muslim women who choose to wear the head scarf in the West, thereby eliciting a cascade of mirror emotions concerning their identity and motives. You fear someone, you are humiliated by someone, and even in the case of hope you are inspired by the success of someone else. Such intertwined, mutually dependent emotions are the key to understanding our identity-dominated world.

Fear, humiliation, and hope thus can be seen as just as natural and vital ingredients in human beings as the three components of blood: red cells, white cells, and plasma. We all require these three elements in order to live in a healthy manner. But health depends on the right balance among them. To have too much or too little of any of these three components is dangerous for the balance of the body and for its long-term health. A balance of emotions is as vital to the "health of the world" as "balanced" blood to the health of individuals.

The two "passions" (emotions) that most concerned the seventeenth-century Dutch philosopher Spinoza were hope and fear, for both relate to uncertainty over what the future will bring. Yet both are necessary in life. An element of fear is necessary for survival, and hope ignites and fuels the motor of life. Even humiliation in very small doses can stimulate one to do better, especially if it comes from a friend who does better in sports or school or a friendly country that performs better in sports or business. But deliberate humiliation without hope is destructive, and too much fear, too much humiliation, and not enough hope constitute the most dangerous of all possible social combinations, the one that leads to the greatest instability and tension.

THE MAPPING OF EMOTIONS

We all might agree that emotions play an important role in human behavior. We might even agree that the emotional conflicts raised by identity issues in today's globalizing world appear likely to have a significant impact on geopolitics. But what is the specific, concrete connection between emotions and geopolitical conflict? Is it possible to go beyond generalizations about emotions to see actual patterns of behavior that help explain what is happening on the world stage?

I believe it is, and that the *mapping of emotions* is one way of recognizing such patterns. Such a mapping involves bringing together elements as diverse as surveys of public opinion (how people feel about themselves, their present, and their future), the statements of political leaders, and cultural productions such as movies, plays, and books. Architecture is particularly significant, for it reflects the way a society decides to project itself in space at a given time. Through indicators like these, emotions, the most subjective of topics, can be approached and studied in an objective, if not in a "scientific," way.

The mapping of resources or interests is of course much more familiar than the mapping of emotions. In fact at one time geopolitics, in the strictest sense of the term, was based on a belief in the absolute determinism of geography, the conviction that the behavior of nations and empires was dictated by their geography. A maritime power like Great Britain would necessarily behave differently from a continental power like Russia. In the hands of certain influential geopolitical thinkers of the first half of the twentieth century this notion became oversimplified. In its worst manifestation, when its ideas influenced Hitler's lebensraum ideology, geopolitics even contributed to the destruction of Europe in the Second World War by encouraging statesmen to view control of territory as crucial enough to national destiny to justify launching a global war.

Today most students of history recognize that while geography does matter, it is not the single determining factor some once claimed. In sixteenth-century France the philosopher Jean Bodin developed a theory of climates that remains useful. Political regimes are still in part influenced by climatic and geographic considerations. The so-called Protestant ethic appears to exert a stronger influence in cold countries than in hot and humid climates, yet Singapore would appear to be a perfect counterexample, where humidity and an ethic of hard work are not incompatible. Like any other form of determinism, geographic determinism fails to reflect the complex realities of human behavior.

Thus, if we are to apply the basic insight that geography influences behavior to the world of emotions, we must avoid the oversimplification and rigid determinism that are the twin pitfalls of such an approach. But if we do not integrate emotions into our analysis of the world, we are in danger of ignoring a fundamental aspect of political life.

For instance, we cannot begin to comprehend the Israeli-Palestinian conflict without understanding its emotional dimension. This is of course a conflict about land, security, prosperity, and sovereignty, but it is also charged with emotions. A leading member of the Palestinian elite once memorably described to me how his people felt: "It is as if you were walking in the streets of the city where you were born and suddenly above your head, a window opens and someone throws out of that window a human being that crushes you as he touches the ground." The unfortunate passerby is of course the Palestinian; the person responsible for the defenestration is the European; and his victim, who in turn becomes the oppressor of the Palestinian, is the Israeli Jew.

No doubt children of Holocaust survivors would find this interpretation of the Palestinian-Israeli conflict difficult to accept. But they have to take it into account if they are to understand the position, the motives, and the concerns of the adversary with whom they must deal.

How do you reconcile two peoples with diverse emotional landscapes, when what is the miracle of rebirth for one is the Naqbah, the catastrophe of defeat and oppression for the other? While for the Israelis their state is the legitimate and necessary manifestation of nationhood, for the Arabs it is an anachronistic demonstration of Western imperialism.

I consider the Israel-Palestine conflict not only, so to speak, the matrix of international relations but the archetypal encounter between two of the primary emotions I describe in this book, humiliation and fear. A nation has been born out of an absolute and unique tragedy; a people has been crushed and oppressed by a victim rendered blind to the suffering of others by the immensity of his own wounds, physical and psychological. Nothing could be more emotional than this tragic encounter taking place on a world stage still dominated by the conflicting guilt of a Western European world torn between the memories of anti-Semitism and colonialism.

The Israeli-Palestinian conflict could well become the epitome of the relationship between the West and the Arab Islamic world as a whole if it is allowed to remain without a solution. If the West does not successfully exit from this vicious encounter between humiliation and fear taking place in the world between itself and the Arab-Islamic fundamentalists, it may be condemned to inexorable decline and a relegation from the center of history to its margins.

And where is hope? I met it in Asia. I came back from my various Asian trips, from Mumbai to Singapore in particular, convinced that the mood gap between Asia and the rest of the world is huge and growing. In the last World Economic Forum in Davos in January 2008, the contrast between the sense of doom and gloom of the Western representatives and the sense of lighthearted resiliency and confidence demonstrated by Asians was striking. (Of course the fact that the leading government of the West, that of the United States, is now financially dependent on vast sums borrowed from the East surely has something to do with the relative confidence of Asian economic leaders as compared with their Western counterparts.) Yesterday's motto, "When America sneezes, the world catches a cold," seemed to have been replaced in Davos by a new formula: "When America catches pneumonia, China and India merely sneeze." And though the world financial crisis we are now experiencing will affect Asia too as it deepens, the ability of the Asians to rebound is probably greater, enhanced by the "hope surplus" their people enjoy.

EMOTIONS VERSUS CIVILIZATIONS

Some observers have said that conflicts among nations today can be best explained not by emotions but rather by broader and deeper cultural patterns. This is the belief most notably articulated by Samuel Huntington in his famous 1993 essay in which he claimed that a clash of civilizations was about to dominate world politics, in which culture, alongside national interest and political ideology, was becoming a geopolitical fault line. He presented a cyclical vision of history, starting from religions and ending with civilizations, after having gone from the clash between states to oppositions between nations and from nations to ideologies.

I have always had serious reservations about Huntington's theory. I think that in his search for a new enemy in order to focus the foreign policy of the United States after the demise of the Soviet empire, Huntington dangerously confused the notion of culture in general, including social and religious beliefs and behaviors, with that of political culture. Are not many in the Asian world also believers in the universal applicability of Western values and practices such as democracy? If so, what does this do to the idea that cultural fault lines are necessarily political and ideological fault lines as well?

There also seems to be no sign of an alliance between Asia and the Islamic world against the West, as Huntington predicted. On the contrary, in the international arena India and China behave more like satisfied status quo powers than irresponsible and dangerous revolutionaries. China and India largely accept the world as it is. The Chinese seem to feel comfortable with the international status quo as long as they can fully control and suppress any attempt at challenging their imperial power (as they seek to do in Tibet) and as long as they are convinced that the tide of world affairs is moving their way. The idea, widespread in the 1990s, that Europe's past could be Asia's future and that military competitions and insecurity have moved from Western Europe to East Asia has not been confirmed by reality. What has moved from West to East is not war but above all economic growth.

In recent years, the truly revolutionary powers in the world have been the two former rivals of the Cold War: Putin and Medvedev's Russia and George W. Bush's America. And the revolutionary nature of these regimes has been driven not by any cultural factors but by emotional ones: Russia's renewed sense of confidence and its recovery from the humiliation it felt in the wake of the Cold War and America's overconfidence in the universal power of its democratic ideal and the unique strength of its military power, an overconfidence that may in fact reflect a deep identity crisis. With the United States trying to change the existing status quo in the Middle East in the name of democracy, and with Russia threatening to change it in the Caucasus in an effort to restore its own imperial status, America and Russia have had more in common than either side would willingly admit.

Self and Other

By focusing on emotions, I am emphasizing a new reality that can be summarized in very simple terms: *In the age of globalization the relationship with the Other has become more fundamental than ever.*

In classical Europe, in the seventeenth and eighteenth centuries, for example, there were so few absolute Others that they were a source of curiosity, treated as conversation pieces or like exotic animals to be collected and exhibited. With the transportation revolution, absolute Others became much more numerous and were enrolled as an important element of our economic or military adventures. Colonial empires came to play a great role in European rivalries. We had taken great care to "civilize" the Others, and the time had come to use them directly for our own benefits. (Just consider the number of North African or black African graves on the battlefields of World War I in the eastern and northern parts of France.)

But while in the nineteenth and even the first half of the twentieth centuries, the Other was no longer a rare curiosity, it had not yet become the absolute Other, forcing us to question our own identities and to challenge our social and political models. At the time of the Cold War, the absolute Other for the Western world came from the Communist system; in intellectual and cultural terms it was the "other side of the West." Today in our global age the absolute Other comes not only from another, non-Western culture but even, in a sense, from a different century, mixing a quasi-tribal mind-set that seems reminiscent of our own Middle Ages with the technological instruments of the present. And the Other not only evokes our past of religious intolerance and warfare but may also incarnate our future. For the West, yesterday non-Westerners could succeed only if they were following the Western model; they would fail if they stuck to their traditions. Today, when we Westerners look eastward, we are all too uncomfortably aware that we may be glimpsing our own future, one that is out of our control.

With the rise of Asia as a challenge and the emergence of fundamentalism as a threat, the West is today confronted with serious questions about its identity. In the age of globalization, relations with the Other have become so central that we are forced to redefine our own essence. Who are we? What makes us so special and different? This task proves to be far more difficult for someone from the West, who is used to interpreting the world in the categories of "us" and "them," than it is for a Chinese or an Indian, who is used to living in parallel worlds, his own and one that is Western dominated.

Most of my Asian friends went through the best Western universities. They have an intimate knowledge of us and our culture. They know what makes us tick, so to speak. By contrast, the "Asian side" of their personality remains largely a mystery to me and my Western friends. In the West, experts on Asia remain too few and too often limited to their field of expertise, be it art, history, or languages. One highly respected specialist in Japan at a major American university told me many years ago that the more she knew about Japanese culture, the less she "really" understood.

Thus the hybrid nature of Asian identity seems much more adaptive to a world in conflict, and therefore more beneficial, than the relative homogeneity we find in the Western world. Because we in the West still tend to see ourselves as central, we are more challenged and even destabilized in our core identity than Asians are. They manage to remain themselves while becoming us.

Many Shades of Gray:
The Difficulties of Mapping Emotions

Another challenge to the notion that emotions can be a key to understanding global conflict might come from the idea that emotions are too inherently subjective, "soft," and indefinable to be truly meaningful. This is an attitude that connects powerfully with the present dominant scientific, positivist mood in academic circles, particularly in the realm of international relations.

I can understand the appeal of this attitude. The more complex the world becomes, the greater the temptation to analyze the international system through the distanced prism of a scientific or pseudoscientific approach. The refusal to be "policy oriented" can be understood from an ethical standpoint; you do not want to be "corrupted" by even distant contact with day-to-day realities, such as the current war in Iraq. But this approach runs the risk of losing any relevance to the real world. Quantitative analysis theories, so popular today in departments of international relations of many of the world's most prestigious universities, may be reassuring in their abstraction, but does their refusal to touch the big questions make sense? (According to one simple metric, the answer is no. In many universities, students react to this abstraction with their feet. They simply desert these departments.)

The fact is that subjective, "soft" realities are essential to understanding geopolitics on even the most rudimentary level.

Consider maps of physical geography. They have a reassuringly objective quality. Plains are green, mountains are brown, and oceans are blue. Of course nature sometimes changes more brutally than political realities. After a tsunami or an earthquake, the color lines of a physical map can change dramatically, introducing more blue where there had been green or brown. And the warming of the planet will most likely accelerate the rhythm of these natural changes; Greenland already has new islands that were until recently thought to be part of its mainland.

By contrast, political and economic maps aren't objective portraits of natural realities but subjective constructions, very often even instruments in the hands of governments. Israel does not exist on most Arab maps. It has been simply erased, like pictures of opponents to the Soviet regime in reworked photographs at the time of Stalin. Judaea and Samaria stand for the West Bank in Israeli maps. Cyprus is shown split in two on Turkish maps, as one on Greek maps. The Gulf is Arabian for Saudi Arabia and Persian for Iran. It would be easy to multiply these examples.

Of course, data like demography, level of wealth, and energy resources can be treated in a more objective, even scientific way, but this isn't always the case. Even figures can be distorted for political purposes, as with the demographic evolution of respective religious minorities in Lebanon or in Bosnia during the Yugoslav wars of the 1990s, or simply hidden, like life expectancy data in the Soviet Union in the 1970s.

The mapping of political regimes is even trickier. In ancien régime Europe, maps kept evolving as a function of wars and alliances that were successively formed and broken and empires that swelled and shrank. Nations were formed and dissolved—for example, Poland, a country that disappeared as an independent state for more than a century between 1795 and 1918 after three partitions among greedy neighbors.

At the time of the Cold War, maps of the international system had a reassuring simplicity. They barely changed from 1945 to 1989. Two blocs confronted each other, and the rest was the so-called nonaligned world. The Soviet bloc was classically shown in red; the Atlantic alliance, generally in blue.

Since the end of the Cold War, political maps have again become more difficult to define. First, a multiplication of states has emerged, especially in Europe and Central Asia, as a result of the disappearance of Yugoslavia, the end of the Soviet empire, and the peaceful reshaping of countries like Czechoslovakia and Germany.

Second, the criteria for selection of colors are even more difficult to define. Where is Russia to be placed now that it is no longer the Soviet Union? In the European West, which probably makes cultural sense, or in the Asian East, which fits its political culture, given its traditional flirtation with "Oriental despotism"? Should democracies be purely defined in function of the quality of the electoral process, with the danger of confusing "illiberal democracies," such as Iran, with old, established democratic countries based on the rule of law? Should religiosity and faith instead be the criteria for classification, with China and Europe in the same secular category, while the United States, India, and the world of Islam form a kind of spiritual and religious bloc? What is the value of a religious map when in a continent like Europe the practice of Christianity is in deep decline, to judge by the number of vocations for the priesthood and church attendance?

It's clear, then, that even the "objective" factors beloved by those who claim a scientific, positivist approach to history are, at bottom, deeply subjective.

Nonetheless, we must acknowledge that mapping emotions is far from easy. If even classical political maps are increasingly difficult to draw, the mapping of emotions can seem like a pure fantasy and perhaps a dangerous illusion, a superficial and potentially dangerous venture based on subjectivity, simplification, and a Manichaean view of the world.

Even the idea of associating colors with emotions is problematic. What would the colors of emotions be? Colors vary with different cultures. Should humiliation be green because it is the color of Islam and because of the common Western expression "green with envy"? Should fear be red and hope blue, or should it be the reverse? How would the American political vocabulary of "red" and "blue" states affect the equation? The color of affliction is black in some countries, white in others.

It would take the genius of a great artist to capture the subtle variations and nuances of colors that characterize the world of emotions. And even a Turner or a Monet would find it impossible to achieve, especially in today's complicated world.

Another reason for the difficulty of mapping emotions is the growing relativity of geography in our global age. For many, geography is no longer a given but a matter of choice. Consider the case of the United Arab Emirates. In geographic terms, they are clearly located in the Middle East. But in psychological, economic, and emotional terms, they are in Asia, having joined the culture of hope very consciously and very deliberately, helped in this process by their unique combination of huge energy resources and smallness in geographic and demographic terms. Their model is clearly and openly Singapore. Dubai is competing with Malaysia for the possession of the tallest tower buildings in the world. Their towers of optimism reaching to the sky are, and are meant to be, an open declaration of confidence in a region otherwise marked by diffidence and violence.

Of course the price of Dubai's culture of hope for the happy few is the miserable life conditions of those who make that geographic and psychological shift possible. But are these mostly immigrant workers worse off than the millions of unemployed people that surround them? At least these migrant workers are able to feed their families left at home, as long as Dubai's prosperity continues. On the whole, the achievements of the emirates should be respected. They represent important testimonials to the human willpower as well as evidence that Islam and modernity are compatible.

If the state of Israel by a magical or divine process of levitation could leave the Middle East, that would satisfy a majority of Israelis, who are eager to join the Asian sphere of prosperity or perhaps to return to Europe, the continent that was the seat of their tragic destiny but also, for centuries, the context of their blossoming successful integration. I still remember the Israeli professor whose family was of German descent who, as we walked in the streets of Berlin at the peak of the second intifada, took out her German passport and sadly, ironically declared, "This passport is my life insurance." In fact the number of Israeli citizens who have left their country for the Federal Republic of Germany more than doubled to more than four thousand in 2006. The number of Israelis residing abroad is becoming a worrisome brain drain factor for the country.

The geographic shift that remains modest in the case of Israel has reached massive proportions in the case of Palestine and Lebanon, not to mention Iraq, which has seen a huge wave of emigration of more than four million people, half of them having simply left their country, torn by civil war, to try to survive in Jordan or Syria, the rest being displaced within Iraq.

This geographic shuffling is not only demographic in nature but also emotional. The Middle East is exporting not only its citizens but also its passions. The "Asianization" of the Gulf countries has for counterpart the "Arabization" of Asian Islam from India to Thailand. Radical emotions stemming from the Middle East have steadily grown in the last fifteen years in the Islamic part of Asia. Can you be a good Muslim if you don't feel like an Arab, behave like an Arab, and share the same concern for the fate of the Palestinians, for the resistance of the "believers in the true faith" against the American and Zionist imperialists? Terrorist groups from Algeria to Saudi Arabia have been financed by "charities" whose support is drawn mainly from Asia, and Muslim minorities from India to Thailand have grown more intolerant as a result of this Arabization in terms of emotions and cultural identifications. From Singapore to China, from India to Malaysia this radicalization of Islam constitutes an object of international worry.

Of course Islamic fundamentalism in Asia is not only the direct result of the Arabization of Muslim emotions but also a creation of South Asia itself. As a country based purely on religion, the only such country in the world other than Israel, Pakistan has become an epicenter of Islamism. Al Qaeda implanted its networks very early on in this part of the world. Today, with its fragile political system, Pakistan is not only becoming the sanctuary of Afghan rebels but also slowly descending into chaos, a matter of grave concern when one considers a country that possesses nuclear weapons. This dual process of Islamization (or even jihadization), one ingrained in Asia, the other imported from the Middle East, and the two reinforcing each other, constitutes a dangerous time bomb ready to explode at any moment. It is a reality acknowledged by the present Malay government, which is now trying to confront this challenge while attempting (without much success) to change its international image after the twenty-two-year reign of Prime Minister Mahathir bin Mohamad, whose regime had been courting Islamism with an explicit use of anti-Semitic arguments.

And the Middle Easternization of the world does not stop in Asia. It reaches the West and in particular the European continent. The Indian doctors who unsuccessfully tried to commit large terrorist attacks in London and Glasgow in the summer of 2007 were a particularly spectacular manifestation of this phenomenon, after the tragic attacks on Madrid in March 2004 and the attacks on London in July 2005. The existence of this India-based network in Great Britain is a sign that India itself is not immune from fundamentalism and more generally that democracy offers no real protection against the extremist temptations of angered and determined minorities.

To recognize the Middle Easternization of parts of the world is one thing. To see the world only through that prism is another. One cannot react to the tragic complexity of the world with simplified generalizations and simplistic answers. What makes a mapping of emotions so difficult is not only the existence of strong crosscurrents and reciprocal influences but the fact that fear, humiliation, and hope are always present in variable proportions, depending upon the continent, the regions, the countries, and above all the period. In other terms, pockets of Asia are present in Europe alongside pockets of the Middle East, one as a positive influence, the other as a potentially dangerous one.

A country like Estonia, for example, one of the most dynamic in Europe, has had until recently an annual GDP growth of over 10 percent, which places it closer to Asia in terms of economic performance than to the rest of Europe. In fact, all of Nordic Europe beyond the Baltic republics, along with Ireland, is more part of the culture of hope than of the culture of fear. In North America the gentle optimism and the remarkable economic and social performances of a country like Canada have more to do with the hope of the new Asians than with the angst of its powerful neighbor, the United States. And within Asia, the continent of hope, we see the largest proportion of underclass people in the world as well as countries plagued by natural disasters (Bangladesh, Indonesia) and spreading violence (Afghanistan, Pakistan, even Tibet). Again, the dangers of simplistic thinking are obvious.

One further difficulty comes from the fact that even geographic concepts such as Asia, the West, and the Middle East are mostly artificial constructions. Asia is to a large extent a Western category, if not an invention of the West. The Japanese do not perceive themselves as Asians and are resented as Japanese by the rest of Asia. Chameleon-like, they imitate the West while remaining probably the most mysterious and impenetrable of all Asians to the Western mind. India is a kind of intermediate zone between Europe and China and between Buddhism and Islam. And what about China, which perceives itself as a center (if not the center) of civilization rather than as part of a larger ensemble?

Even the notion of the West itself is becoming largely artificial, especially as seen from the West itself. In reality should we not be speaking of two Wests, an American-dominated one and a European-led one, the two in danger of becoming more and more estranged culturally and politically?

Meanwhile the Middle East seems to be expanding, stretching from Algeria, Tunisia, and Morocco in the west to Pakistan and Afghanistan in the east. Yet it is also more than ever an extremely divided reality. Iranians have nothing to do with Arabs or for that matter with Turks. Turkey in its present geography is undeniably Asian, while Turkish elites, mostly perceived as Asian Muslims by a majority of Europeans, proclaim themselves European and want to join the European Union.

Self-perceptions are not necessarily reality. Again, we can look to the global sports arena for some significant indicators. In sports like soccer or basketball, Israel is considered part of Europe, a situation that Israelis enjoy but that does not favor their regional integration within the Middle East. At the same time, no one—least of all the Europeans themselves—considers the classification of Israeli athletes as "Europeans" any kind of first step toward the integration of Israel within the European Union.

WHY EMOTIONS MATTER

The difficulties of dividing the world into regions based on emotional patterns are obviously enormous. Nevertheless, one can attempt to draft a global map of emotions because dominant emotions, like dominant colors in painting, do exist. Even if shades of gray are everywhere, they are lighter in the Asia that succeeds, darker in the Western world, and nearly black in some parts of the Middle East. It is one task of governments to study the emotions of their respective peoples, to capitalize on them if they are positive, to try to reverse or contain them if they are negative. These duties can't be met without one's first attempting to diagnose the emotional state of the population.

Like the seasons, emotions are cyclical. These cycles can be long or short, depending on the culture, on world events, on economic and political developments. In our modern world even a major sports victory can create a sense of elation that may be short-lived but have serious immediate consequences. The Chinese banked on the 2008 Beijing Olympics to confirm the international status of their country, even if the Olympics are the result and not the cause of this status.

Emotions reflect the degree of confidence that a society has in itself. It is this degree of confidence that in turn determines the ability of a society to rebound following a crisis, to respond to a challenge, to adjust to changing circumstances. It is because of the importance of emotions in the collective psyche of peoples that I assume, for example, that China and India have a greater capability to rebound from the present economic crisis than Europe.

Most important, emotions can be changed. Fear can give way to hope. A large part of Barack Obama's appeal as a presidential candidate was his readiness to be a leader who could reopen a cycle of positive emotions in America, reflected in Americans' self-perception and their perception by the rest of the world. By contrast, in France today, workers, industrialists, businessmen, and bankers all are simultaneously collapsing in a mood of pessimism, while the political discourse seems nearly empty in its voluntaristic display of hope.

This fact is at the heart of my argument for the analysis of emotions in the geopolitical arena: Emotions matter. They impact the attitudes of peoples, the relationships between cultures, and the behavior of nations. Neither political leaders nor students of history nor ordinary concerned citizens can afford to ignore them. Attempting to map the emotional patterns of our world may be a perilous exercise, but pretending these patterns do not exist would be more perilous still.

Chapter Two

The Culture of Hope

If we try our best and work hard, the future is beautiful. I came here to build a new society. The people here need houses. I am making money but we do not come here just for money. Thirty years ago China was like Angola; it was not good but now it is more beautiful.

—XUEBAO DING, A CHINESE WORKER IN ANGOLA,
QUOTED IN ALEC RUSSELL, "THE NEW COLONIALISTS,"
FINANCIAL TIMES, NOVEMBER 17–18, 2007

Hope is confidence.
In the Western world the notion of hope has two different connotations. There is hope in the spiritual sense of the term, the belief in the salvation of humanity through the redemption from sin. But there is also the secular meaning of the term. Hope is trust in one's identity, in one's ability to interact positively with the world. The words of the Chinese worker in Angola that serve as the opening to this chapter are a nearly perfect postmodern illustration of the secular significance of hope. Hope is the opposite of resignation, a form of trust that

pushes us to move toward others, to accept without fear how they differ from us.

Is there a lesson to be drawn from the fact that hope has moved from West to East, from a Christian-dominated world to a largely pantheistic world where secularism predominates (as in China) or where spirituality has stopped being an obstacle to growth (as in India)? Not for nothing is one of the best recent studies on India's miracle (written by Edward Luce) titled *In Spite of the Gods: The Rise of Modern India*.

Hope has not only moved east but also taken on a materialist, secular overtone, as the spiritual meaning of the word dwindles in salience. In the twenty-first century, hope is based on doing better in this world here and now, not on the belief in some future better world, either on earth or in heaven. In spite of the traditional belief in reincarnation so powerful throughout Asia, a growing number of Chinese, Indians, and other Asians now feel driven to do as well as possible, individually and collectively, during their present earthly passage, as if they have come under the influence of the so-called Protestant ethic, which drove the growth of the West (demonstrating, by the way, that secular hope already existed in Europe in the eighteenth and nineteenth centuries).

Hope today is about economic and social empowerment, and its chief dwelling place is in the East. What's more, for significant numbers of Asians, what counts is not only that they seek to catch up with the West, but that they are confident they can and will do it. If faith is "a hope in the unseen," the Asian world is steadily moving beyond faith, putting their hope in the material progress they can see, feel, hear, taste, and experience in the rapidly changing world around them.

ASIAN HOPE

Consider for a moment the skyline of Pudong, the newly developed district of Shanghai that is rapidly becoming a financial hub for all China. Before 1990 where these proud towers are now standing, there were mainly farm fields. Today the place is booming with energy. The architectural style chosen by the city planners conveys an impression of modernity and confidence, of optimism in the future. The architects, mostly Chinese but including a few Westerners, have been given (within the limits of a very tight political system) a blank check and the exhortation "Be inventive, be daring, be tall—in sum, be modern." The result is a gleaming array of futuristic spires as breathtaking as any in the world: the tiered, 88-story Jin Mao Tower; the Shanghai World Financial Center (the second-tallest skyscraper in the world); the distinctive Oriental Pearl Tower (with its three massive columns supporting eleven suspended spheres of varying sizes); and the latest addition, Shanghai Center, a supertall skyscraper now under construction that will ultimately soar 580 meters (127 stories) into the sky. This is twenty-first-century architecture—often at its best, sometimes at its worst, but never less than audacious.

The Pudong skyline does not represent the last gasp of an outdated style, like the Paris Opéra, built by Charles Garnier for Napoleon III, a testimonial to the inflated ego of an empire about to crumble based on a reinvention of the classical style of the ancien régime. Nor does it mimic the heavy and grandiloquent style of Russian architecture under Putin. It is something new that consciously celebrates the confluence of two approaches to modernity, Western and Asian. It is the visual proof that modernity can no longer be equated with Westernization, a sign of another school of modernity coming out of Asia.

Move from architecture to operas. Monkey: Journey to the West, an opera based on The Journey to the West, a classical masterpiece of Chinese literature, was presented during the 2007–2008 season in Manchester, Paris, and Berlin, in a version that is the ultimate synthesis of Western pop music, Chinese dance and circus traditions, and above all modernity. The show can be described as a cultural UFO of the global age, or as one of many preliminary symbols of a new cultural age. It is especially a demonstration of confidence by a China that no longer hesitates to submit its classical texts to the most modern treatment combining Western and Chinese influences. Thus it is a throwback to an earlier, self-confidently imperial China, the China of the eighteenth century, whose emperors felt confident enough to permit Chinese artists to create paintings and drawings in the "Jesuit" (Western) style. It is the insecure country that feels the need to shield itself from foreign influences. Confidence and cultural openness are intertwined. (The cultural confidence of modern China, however, has its limits. When one of the best-known Chinese actresses, Zhang Ziyi, played a Japanese prostitute in Hollywood's *Memoirs of a Geisha*, the reactions were far from positive. Many claimed she demeaned China and went too far by playing such a role in an American movie.)

Let us move to the world of fashion, where the influence of young Asian designers—Japanese, Chinese, and especially Indians—has been growing rapidly. For the first time in Paris in the fall of 2007, an Indian stylist (Manish Arora) opened Fashion Week with a show that fused modernity and popular Indian imagery. These fashion parades represent in yet another way the crisscrossing of influences among cultures that have gained or regained so much confidence that they can welcome fusion with other cultures. The Indians and Chinese no longer need to be culturally defensive (or, for that matter, offensive); they can simply be themselves, the unique products of mixed influences between them and us. They acknowledge what they owe the West but realize proudly that we in the West have also been changed by our mutual encounter.

It's instructive to consider how cultural cross-fertilization has changed in recent decades. Asian influence, particularly Chinese, helped shape the fashionable rococo style of eighteenth-century Europe; the impressionist painters and symbolist poets of late-nineteenth-century Europe were very much under the influence of Japan. At that time Asia represented poetry for Europe, while Europe represented modernity for Asia. Now this equation has been reversed, with Asia exemplifying the future while Europe stands for a glorious but fading past. This turnabout raises significant questions for both continents. Will Europe become predominantly a museum in Asian eyes? Is Asia losing its uniqueness as a result of globalization, even as it moves to take the dominant position in shaping the world's culture once claimed by the West?

There is also a new sense of balance between the West and Asia. Consider the field of medicine, where Chinese traditional techniques such as acupuncture now happily coexist with modern Western practices, not only in Asia but in a growing number of hospitals, clinics, and medical offices throughout Europe and America. Or look at the popularity of Bollywood movies in the Western world, which has mushroomed to the point where Indian stars are helping revive the musical comedy film genre in the West. For the last twenty-nine years (in the case of China) and the last eighteen years (in the case of India), these two powerhouses have been growing economically at almost 10 percent per year. The Indian journalist and politician Jairam Ramesh coined the term "Chindia" as a quick and easy way to refer to the two rapidly growing demographic giants of Asia.

It's a handy term, but also a deeply ambivalent concept. China and India are not in the same category in terms of economic weight. Measured by population, GDP, and other standard indicators, China is twice as powerful as India. Yet if one adds the more than 350 million Chinese who have climbed to middle-class status to the more than 350 million Indians who have accomplished the same thing, they add up to the greatest emerging giant in the world, an entity of more than 700 million people who are transforming the international economic and even strategic order. Chindia refers to these 700 million. The question is whether they are a sufficiently strong locomotive to pull the remaining hundreds of millions who inhabit their homelands out of poverty and massive inequality.

In a broader sense, Chindia refers to two very different civilizations that feel both sufficiently strong and self-confident to open themselves to the world and submit their cultural essence to the test of others. Yet the self-confidence of Chindia is selective. In the case of China, it does not extend to the political field—understandably, since China's leaders have no real understanding of the meaning of freedom and democracy and their contradictory allegiances to both communism and capitalism are probably untenable even in the short run. Nor does it extend to the control and management of China's "imperial policy." The brutal repression in Tibet in the spring of 2008 expressed the near panic of Chinese leaders at the risk of seeing similar explosions in other parts of their empire.

In fact we see in China the coexistence of two brands of nationalism: a defensive nationalism, which insists on shutting down any activity that might threaten the empire, and a positive nationalism, beaming with optimism and confidence. (According to a recent Pew survey, the Chinese are the most optimistic people in the world.)

Nor does Chindia's self-confidence embrace the poor masses, who despite their vast numbers do not define the mood or the direction of either country, but who could, if they were to become desperate, derail the logic of hope throughout the region.

Nevertheless, as long as the sense of progress among the rising millions transcends the despair, anger, and hunger of the poor majority, then the culture of hope will prevail in Chindia. And not only there. The region of hope also includes the members of the ASEAN group (Association of Southeast Asian Nations, now including Cambodia, Brunei, Laos, Thailand, Indonesia, Malaysia, Burma, Vietnam, and the Philippines, and the 2008 leader of the group, Singapore). In an uneven and unbalanced way, they too are progressing; they have surmounted the financial crash of 1998 and their respective political turbulence with a sense of pride and dedication and a sane sense of emulation addressed toward their prosperous neighbors: "We too can do it. We will show you."

Of course to describe an entire continent under a single rubric, the continent of hope, is inevitably somewhat provocative and perhaps simplistic. Let's consider some caveats and provisos that must be taken seriously.

First, as we've already noted, the very concept of Asia is largely a Western one. Asians do not naturally call themselves or consider themselves Asians—at least not nearly to the extent that Europeans consider themselves Europeans. Asians do not have a common religion in the same way the Europeans share the complex (and now somewhat diluted) fusion of Greek, Jewish, and Roman religious cultures in what is called Christianity. They do not have a common history. They do not have a common enemy (which is what Islam once represented for the Christian nations of Europe). They do not have common cultural references. For example, in the Chinese tale already mentioned, *The Journey to the West*, the "West" referred to is India. It is perhaps significant that it is the small city-state of Singapore, which uses English as its common official language to unite its Chinese, Malay, and Indian populations, that has the only Museum of Asian Civilization in Asia.

Second, the culture of hope does not embrace all the countries of Asia. As I'll explain, the important country of Japan has, so to speak, gone beyond the brand of hope now embraced by the rest of the continent, while numerous other countries, from Pakistan to the Philippines, are not yet there.

In Pakistan, for example, one of the most contradictory and problematic countries of the world, there is, at the level of the elites and of a small nascent middle class, something like a streak of modernity and a sense of what is needed to go beyond fundamentalism and violence and to integrate the country into the Asian culture of hope. But this awareness is shared by just a small segment of the population. Pakistan is one of the most worrisome countries in the world, not only because it is a nuclear power but because it gives the impression of being on the verge of political implosion. When you walk the streets of Karachi, you feel far away from the hopeful Asia of Beijing or Delhi.

By contrast with Pakistan, North Korea seems slightly less dangerous today, even if it looks more like the victim of a brutal and cynical political sect than a vessel of hope. As for Burma (Myanmar), in spite of its rich natural resources, it has been dragged down the ladder of growth and prosperity by the oppressive, corrupt, and systematic mismanagement of its brutal military junta, becoming an Asian equivalent of Robert Mugabe's Zimbabwe.

In the spring of 2008, Burma and China both were faced with dramatic challenges from nature—the cyclone in Burma, the earthquake in China. Their reactions could not have been more different. The responsible behavior of the Chinese was in perfect contrast with the incompetent, despotic brutality of the military junta in Myanmar. Of course the Chinese saw in the catastrophe, coming as it did on the eve of the Olympic Games, an opportunity to redress their image so damaged by the events of Tibet. The government's attempts to silence the voices from civil society demanding investigation into the shoddily built schools where Chinese children died may signify a swing of the pendulum back toward repression.

If there is hope in Myanmar, we see it in the heroic defiance offered by opposition leader and Nobel prizewinner Aung San Suu Kyi and the spiritual resistance of the Buddhist priests. It is a country that has managed to isolate itself from international influences almost completely; that is why sanctions against Myanmar should not focus so much on isolating the regime as on exposing its leaders to the realities of the world outside their national ghetto.

So it must be understood from the outset that our description of Asia as the continent of hope, including countries like the Philippines and Indonesia, which are at the fringes of hope, given their noticeable yet still incomplete economic progress, is one-sided and slightly exaggerated, yet fundamentally accurate.

THE RETURN OF THE MIDDLE EMPIRE

When one speaks of Asia as the continent of hope, it is clearly China and India that come to mind. Their dual economic rise as the two demographic giants of the planet has been remarkable in spite of their equally gigantic shortcomings. Yet each country constitutes in itself a unique and very different case.

"China is back" was the explicit message of an exhibit titled "The Three Emperors" organized under the auspices of the Chinese government at the Royal Academy of Arts in London in 2005. The centerpiece of the exhibit was a huge painting in the European ("Jesuit") style familiar in eighteenth-century China, depicting a parade of European envoys paying tribute to the Chinese emperor. The message could not be clearer: "You too will soon pay tribute to us." In today's China of course there is no emperor, just a bland, enigmatic, and mildly competent bureaucracy under the leadership of Hu Jin Tao. But there is a tremendous sense of pride and confidence over what China was yesterday and what it is becoming again.

On my first trip to China in 1985 the first monument I was required to see was a gigantic dam across the Yangtze River. "We were the first people in history to have mastered the art of the dam," was the first message my guide from the diplomatic service wanted to convey to me. More surprisingly, he also conveyed to me his deep frustration with his life. He considered himself a failure and nearly exploded with rage when he accompanied me back to my luxury hotel for foreigners and saw that my room was bigger than the apartment he lived in with his entire family. "I made the crucial mistake of joining the diplomatic service," he told me, "rather than becoming a businessperson."

To this day I wonder what has happened to him. Has he fulfilled his capitalist dream?

This contrast between pride and frustration constituted my first impression of China in the mid-1980s. Today both emotions continue to run high in China, for frustration is in its own way a by-product of hope: The more you progress, the more you demand and expect.

To understand the particular nature of the Chinese psyche, the difference between China and Egypt may be enlightening. Both the Chinese and Egyptian civilizations were among the oldest and richest in the world. But high Egyptian civilization disappeared long ago (despite attempts by contemporary Egyptian leaders to evoke those past glories as a way of claiming current relevance and importance). By contrast, traditional Chinese civilization still exists, unique and largely unchanged, having passed the test of time. This continuity is a source of both problems and creativity.

China has always been the most populous country on earth. As a result, the fear of social and economic chaos has always obsessed China's leaders. In reaction, they have created a system where individuals have always had to submit to a collective logic rather than a personal one.

China's size influenced its national psychology in another important way. The self-perception of China as the Middle Empire implied not simply geographic centrality but also the conviction that China was in some way the center of gravity of the universe. Unlike Russia (for example), this immense and self-confident empire did not have to expand to exist. The Great Wall made China a sanctuary, but it also expressed the fact that China did not need to conquer others to feel important. China did expand, of course, but its territorial growth was driven not so much by the force of arms as by demographics, the sheer numbers of Chinese, used by the regime as a colonizing and controlling force. Recently, for example, China has encouraged a large influx of Han Chinese to Tibet and Xinjiang, where China fears pan-Turkic and pan-Islamist subversion. The demographic card is also being played by China in Central Asia, where, according to Professor Harry G. Gelber, quoting unofficial estimates, by 2004 there were already as many as three hundred thousand Chinese, mainly merchants, in Kazakhstan alone. (Recently, however, with the growth of the Chinese economy, the number of Chinese in Siberia seems to be diminishing. Job opportunities, it seems, are now available in greater numbers in the Chinese homeland.)

Another dimension to this demographic card is of a softer, cultural nature. Chinese influence in the world is multiplied by the strong role played by the Chinese diaspora, the millions of ethnic Chinese and their descendants who have established powerful footholds in business, culture, and politics around the world, primarily in Southeast Asia but also well beyond. The diaspora can be counted on by Beijing, especially in the current period of economic growth and national pride, as a precious relay of influence and as a vector of business deals.

Thus, from the strict standpoint of territorial expansionist ambitions, the comparisons often made by Western analysts between China today and Germany at the end of the nineteenth century do not really apply. The rivalry among China, India, and Japan will not shape the future of Asia as the rivalry among Great Britain, France, Russia, and Germany shaped Europe (and the world) in the nineteenth and early twentieth centuries, nor will the Asians tear themselves to pieces through nationalistic warfare, as some Western commentators believe. The differences between Germany then and China now are much greater than the similarities. Newly united Germany was a power in a hurry, especially after the departure of the influential chancellor Bismarck (who was the only man capable of exercising restraint on Emperor Wilhelm II). It was both overconfident and insecure. China, by contrast, is a reemerging empire whose sense of time is infinitely longer than ours in the West. Far from being overconfident, it is deeply aware of the huge challenges and contradictions it has to surmount and of its manifold vulnerabilities.

If one seeks a nineteenth-century European analogy for contemporary China, I suggest one look not at Germany but at the exhortation given to the French citizens by François Guizot, the prime minister of King Louis-Philippe: "Get rich and be quiet." But what happens when this "contract" is broken? Will the Chinese keep quiet if they no longer get rich?

Yet despite China's awareness of its vulnerabilities, it remains convinced that time is on its side. This conviction was reinforced both by the events of 9/11 and by the American reaction to hyperterrorism. That reaction has accelerated "the return of Authoritarian Great Powers," Israeli military historian Azar Gat has argued powerfully in *Foreign Affairs*. China believes not only that the soft power of America has been hurt by the Bush administration's behavior but also that its own soft power has been boosted by the growing skepticism about democracy and human rights, values that America preaches but often fails to practice.

The rise of economically successful and nondemocratic countries such as China and Russia is a proof for Beijing that its authoritarian approach represents a viable alternative path to modernity. In their dealings with the African continent, the Chinese are poised to advance this message to African regimes: "Unlike our counterparts in America and Europe, we are not a former colonial power spouting hypocritical lessons about democracy and human rights. Nor are we a new imperial power from the East. Instead we are dealing with you in a matter-of-fact way. We need your natural resources to keep growing, and you need our money to start growing. Let's work together for mutual benefit."

At the same time, it's clear that the new Chinese middle classes and the wealthy want to live in Western style. In fact the world's biggest economic, ecological, and perhaps political challenge comes from the fact that 1.3 billion Chinese would like to live and spend like Westerners without necessarily being governed like them. They love our music, our films, our food (including, increasingly, our ecologically risky meat diets), and our clothes. But in so many other ways they do not want to become like us, even if they do not know exactly what they do want to become or what kind of international role they want to play.

The great question is whether China's ambivalent and hybrid approach, in which Western capitalism and individual economic ambitions coexist with Eastern-style authoritarianism, is realistic. In the short term, it may continue to be successful. But in the long term, it spells trouble. China needs the rule of law as well as hardheaded mercantilism. It was the absence of the rule of law and the resulting corruption that led to the sacrifice of thousands of children when their schools collapsed upon them during the earthquake of 2008. There is a limit to how many such disasters China's people will accept.

The arrogance of the Chinese regime has also been creating problems on the international scene. The Chinese attitude toward the repression led by the Burmese generals in the fall of 2007 has been, to say the least, less than helpful. China is the only country in the world that can exert real pressure on Myanmar, yet it deliberately failed to use its clout, at least not in any visible fashion. In the same manner, China's vicious reaction to the reception offered in 2007 by the United States to the Dalai Lama of Tibet was neurotic, demeaning to the regime, and detrimental to the image of China in the world. And one senses something like a competitive irresponsibility between Russia and China in their attitudes toward Ahmadinejad's Iran, in spite of the complex ambivalence of their positions. In Africa we see still more examples of China's cynical short-term calculations, the principle of noninterference leading to an implicit criminal complicity with the regime of Omar Hassan al-Bashir in Sudan (in spite of its grave violations of human rights in Darfur) and with the murderous regime of Mugabe in Zimbabwe. China badly needs a new elite animated by a sense of the common good if it is to remain a stable country and to become one day a positive and responsible stakeholder in world affairs or even a benevolent superpower.

Nevertheless, there are small signs that China is beginning

to grow into its new role as a great power on the world stage. The return of Hong Kong to China in the mid-1990s proceeded more smoothly than most observers expected. The Chinese leaders have demonstrated sufficient intelligence to balance Hong Kong's semi-Western level of freedom with the need for control by the Chinese authorities. Chinese leaders have played a globally positive role in the so far successful attempt to resolve the North Korean nuclear crisis: They managed to prevent a collapse of North Korea, which could have led to a reunified and stronger Korea and brought a flood of refugees pouring across China's borders, and they have significantly curbed North Korea's nuclear ambitions.

Furthermore, in helping create the Shanghai Group (along with Russia, Kazakhstan, Kyrgyzstan, Tajikistan, and Uzbekistan), the Chinese seem to be playing a balancing role in the style of nineteenth-century Europe, helping offset Western influence in Central Asia with a stabilizing Asian counterforce and doing so in a much more prudent manner than their nineteenth-century counterparts. In the words of Zbigniew Brzezinski, President Carter's former national security adviser (quoted by Harry Gelber), "There is no doubt that China is quietly creating a very successful coprosperity sphere in East Asia. The countries of the region increasingly are paying China due deference, something to which the Chinese graciously respond."

Thus it would be a gross misreading of the international situations and of Chinese thinking to see China only as a disturbing and threatening factor. And we should not measure China solely according to its commitment to democracy. The absence of democratic accountability and the lack of any real understanding of the rule of law are above all a problem for the Chinese themselves. We cannot and must not impose our categories on them. We in the West have to consider what they do at least in part through their eyes and in a multidimensional, not unidimensional, way, without ever forgetting and forfeiting our values. It is a difficult balancing exercise, which implies a sensitivity to diplomatic nuance not always demonstrated by Western leaders, who end up awkwardly pinned by the contradictions between their human rights rhetoric and their defense of national commercial interests.

The lack of freedom and the absence of an independent judiciary system constitute serious brakes on the Chinese path to long-term economic growth and sustainable ecological development. But the immense majority of Chinese judge their leaders with different criteria in mind. They want material progress, more decent housing conditions, and the freedom to travel abroad (which certainly takes precedence for most Chinese over the freedom to think, write, and publish dissent). After a century of suffering through deprivation and scarcity, disorder and insecurity, all exacerbated by a surfeit of ideology, most Chinese want a period of political rest. But they also expect their state to protect them from the violence of nature, from man-made pollution, and even from the brutal behavior of corrupt and inefficient local officials. These demands inevitably have political consequences.

Nonetheless, political change is very slowly coming, driven mainly not by outside pressure but by internal factors, including the demands of an increasingly self-assertive middle class.

Chinese citizens are also starting to demand more from their authorities. The picture of the woman who stood up for her house a few years ago to oppose its destruction made world news, and her photo became a modern symbol of civic resistance, a twenty-first-century equivalent of the young student facing down a tank on Tiananmen Square in May 1989. Of course both lost—the house was destroyed, and the student movement was crushed—but in the near future the next such symbol of opposition may be victorious.

While traveling in the heart of China in the summer of 2006, my older son witnessed some early signs of an emerging Chinese civil society. Travelers who had had their flight between two Chinese cities canceled as the result of the incompetence of the Chinese air company organized a kind of demonstration. The representative of the airline not only "lost face" but was forced to grant financial compensation to the stranded passengers. Similarly, after the tragedy of Sichuan, bereaved parents did call for justice and not just for financial compensations.

The current combination between economic progress and political stagnation will last as long as hope prevails. For hope implies above all the continued pursuit of economic growth.

In reality, the Chinese do not think they have to do much internationally in order to continue to grow in terms of prestige, influence, and authority. They simply have to go on reaping the benefits of the mistakes made by others, especially what they and many perceive as the American overreaction to Islamic fundamentalism. One day, as events dictate, they will enjoy their moment of emergence on the international diplomatic stage, as the United States emerged in 1905, when it organized the San Francisco conference that ended the Russo-Japanese War. China is patiently waiting for its own equivalent.

The chief stumbling blocks that could stymie the patient Chinese plan are of course Taiwan and Tibet. The issues at stake are very different. Tibet is ruled by China in a heavy-handed manner, while Taiwan is, for all practical purposes, fully independent from Beijing under the formula "One state, two systems."

The rise of China seems likely to lead inevitably to an eclipse of American influence. America may, for better or worse, remain the key actor in Europe and the Middle East. But when one looks at the 2008 North Korean and Myanmar crises, one wonders whether this is still true in East Asia. It appears that China, not the United States, is becoming to East Asia what Great Britain was for Europe through most of the nineteenth century: the great balancer. Of course the spectacular rise of China has led the other Asian countries, Japan in particular, to do their best to balance China, for China (unlike Great Britain) is a continental power with possible expansionist temptations.

In its attempt to stem the growth of Chinese power, the United States is counting on two main cards. The first is its hope that market-driven economic growth will force China to accept democratic moderation, even if it does not become a full-fledged democracy. The second is the influence of India. At the peak of the transatlantic crisis over Iraq in 2003, a top American diplomat remarked triumphantly to me, "We may have lost five hundred million Europeans, but we have gained more than one billion Indians. The first are in a process of decay, but the second are emerging as a new force in the world." Let us turn now to India and see whether these American hopes for a benevolent Indian influence in Asia are warranted.

THE EMERGENCE OF INDIA

If "China is back," India is arriving on the world stage for the first time. It does not feel like an old empire recovering its central status, but like a new nation celebrating (in 2008) the sixtieth anniversary of its independence with a combination of immense pride and deep self-questioning: "We did so much so quickly, but have we done it the right way?"

Certainly the task of creating a new nation in the vast subcontinent was daunting. Is there another country where one encounters such an extraordinary mixture of ethnic groups, languages, religions, and cultural practices? Winston Churchill used to say of India that it was "merely a geographical expression. It is no more a single country than the Equator." Yet India has proved Churchill wrong. It is much more than the sum of its contradictions. It may once have been merely a myth and an idea, yet now it has become a very pragmatic reality.

If India lacks China's history as a great imperial power, it nonetheless has a rich and powerful tradition in a very different realm. Sixty years ago in libraries around the world, books about India were to be found mainly under the "spirituality" category, not under "economics" or "politics." The wealth of India was of a "spiritual nature"; economist Amartya Sen reminds us that the Chinese in the first millennium CE classically referred to India as the "Buddhist kingdom." He reminds us also, in *The Argumentative Indian: Writings on Indian History, Culture and Identity*, that it was Ashoka, a Buddhist emperor of India, who, in the third century BCE, "not only outlined the need for toleration and the richness of heterodoxy, but also laid down what are perhaps the oldest rules for conducting debates and disputations, with the opponents duly honoured in every way on all occasions." This tradition of tolerance formed a sharp contrast not only with China but also at the time with Europe.

The inheritance of Gandhi's legacy of nonviolence extended this unique dimension of Indian culture to the political realm. It is difficult to assess what's left of Gandhi's inheritance today. In October 2007 Arte, the Franco-German television channel, featured a program entitled *On Gandhi's Path* that contained a laughing competition named after Gandhi. So much for the profound teachings and political lessons of Gandhi. The same program showed how, in nearly all Indian villages, the omnipresent busts of Gandhi have now been deposited in municipal garages. It is as if India, in a deliberate fit of "realism," had turned its back on him.

Similarly, when India was the guest star country at the World Economic Forum in Davos, it celebrated with elaborate fashion shows and other glitzy symbols of stylish capitalist consumption. It was difficult to imagine that a half-naked philosopher and political activist who preached simplicity and austerity was the father of this new nation.

So India's inner contradictions are at least as deep as China's, but they are of a different nature. Indians are legitimately proud of their democratic status. The Indian formula "the largest democracy in the world" is as ritualized as the Chinese claim to be "the oldest civilization in the world." But this pride coexists with disgust over the incompetence and corruption of India's political class—the worst in the world, according to many Indian intellectuals. Of course free elections, an independent judiciary, and a free press do matter, but these assets are seriously weakened by the eroding force of corruption. What is the meaning of democracy without a properly functioning rule of law?

The other major flaw of Indian democracy is its unique caste system. Disturbingly, it seems that the battle against class divisions (including the caste system) has weakened in India in recent years. Not only has Nehru's dream of establishing a social system free of class stratification barriers not come true, but it seems to be slowly evaporating, victim of the nonseriousness of the political elites in power and the greed of the capitalist classes, which are more obsessed with economic growth than with social justice.

Rich Indians tend not even to see the huge masses who live in poverty. Their selective eyes go across or above them with a serenity of mind that may be at least in part due to the existence of the caste system. The implicit attitude is: Of course they are very poor, but what can you expect? It has always been like this, and at least there are fewer of them today, and they don't die of starvation any longer.

It is true that absolute poverty has decreased significantly in India. Today fewer than 10 percent of the population live in absolute poverty, as compared to 25 percent two decades ago. Yet the problem of poverty is far from solved, and it is distressing to see the Indian elites taking an attitude of indifference toward it.

During the celebrations of India's sixtieth anniversary, Prime Minister Manmohan Singh addressed this problem, emphasizing the need not so much for a continuation of economic growth as for much greater fairness in distributing the benefits from economic progress. In fact the denunciations of social injustice offered by the Indian prime minister and the Chinese premier sounded very much alike, as if they wanted to reinforce the validity of the concept of Chindia—in this case, a Chindia that demands greater social justice even as most societal energies are focused on the pursuit of economic growth.

India demonstrates that modernity does not automatically bring about greater equality. Perhaps modernity is even exacerbating the country's less savory traditions. For example, as Edward Luce has noted, the gender gap between boys and girls in India has sharply increased. Modernity also seems to be intensifying the roles of nationalism and religion in politics. Bloody communal riots have once again broken out across India, killing more than two thousand Muslims in 2003. And in 2008 the spectacular terrorist attack on Mumbai, which was perceived by many Indians as their own 9/11, demonstrated both the vulnerability and the resiliency of India. To resolve these problems, neither a secularized Europe nor a materialistic China provides a model for India. If there is a model, it is much more the United States, with its (mostly) stable combination of secularized, nonsectarian religion and inclusive patriotism, symbolized by the unofficial national motto "In God We Trust." But can India develop an ethic based on the implicit motto "In *Gods* We Trust"?

In comparative terms, there is probably more hope and less despair in India than in China. Very rich Indians are amazed by what they have been able to achieve in such a short period of time and by the international respect they have attained. Nonetheless, unlike the Chinese, the Indians seem deeply uncertain about their new identity as an emerging giant. They appear to derive the confidence they need to assume their new status in the world from the respect, if not envy, that the rest of the world feels for their economic dynamism and success. At the May 2008 President's Conference in Jerusalem marking the sixtieth anniversary of the creation of the state of Israel, there were two "stars." The obvious, visible star was the president of the United States, George W. Bush; the more discreet one was Lakshir Mittal, the giant steel company that is a symbol of India's coming-of-age in the world of globalization.

Beyond India there is the Indian diaspora, which numbers around twenty million. Its members are increasingly successful and assertive, deriving confidence, pride, and even a sense of personal legitimacy from India's rising international status. Today Indian financial analysts are highly sought after in New York and London; Indian physicians are prized staff members at the leading medical centers in the United States; and an Indian-American (albeit a Christian), Piyush "Bobby" Jindal, now serving as governor of Louisiana, was even mentioned as a potential vice presidential candidate during the 2008 election cycle.

The rising confidence of upper-middle-class Indians, whether in India or elsewhere in the world, has for counterpart the fabled "resilience" that Pavan K. Varma describes in his book *Being Indian* as a quality derived from centuries of adversity. "No foreigner can ever understand the extent to which an Indian is mentally prepared to accept the unacceptable," writes Varma. As long as belief in change keeps the many marginalized peripheries engaged, hope will prevail in India.

If China's confidence is based partially on its imperial past, India's is based on its vision of the future. A youthful nation (with 700 million out of 1.1 billion under the age of twenty-five), India is "the 1 percent society": In the words of T. N. Ninan, one of the country's most respected editors (quoted by Edward Luce), "Whichever indicator you choose, whether it is economic or social, India is improving at a rate of roughly 1 percent a year." "To judge by the living conditions of Indians," continues Luce, "and not by the drama of national events, the country is moving forward on a remarkably stable trajectory." Yet to keep growing, India must develop its infrastructure, reduce inequality, and curb corruption.

In comparative terms, the complex diversity of pluralist India may be one of the key reasons for the survival and stability of its democracy. By contrast, China's centralized nature makes it much more efficient but also much more vulnerable to the rapid spread of chaos if political instability were to mount.

THE JAPANESE EXCEPTION

If the two-headed giant Chindia represents the full flowering of Asian hope, what about the other great Asian economic powerhouse, Japan? Why is that affluent island nation not also a full-fledged participant in the culture of hope? Let's take a brief detour to examine the circumstances that make Japan the major exception among the nations of Asia.

Japan of course pioneered the Asian economic miracle as early as the mid-1960s. The Tokyo Olympics in 1964 celebrated the Japanese renaissance less than twenty years after the end of World War II and more than forty years before the Olympic Games came to Beijing.

A chameleon-like country that in its insularity is probably more mysterious and more difficult to apprehend for a Western mind than either China or India, Japan is living proof that modernity and Westernization cannot be equated. Japan is also perceived as "Asian" only by the West. In Asia today, Japan, more than sixty years after the end of World War II, is still resented as uniquely, arrogantly "Nippon" by the majority of its neighbors. Too Western for the majority of Asians, the Japanese have remained too Asian to be fully understood by Westerners.

One of the key reasons for the divorce still existing between Japan and the rest of Asia is of course history and the scars of the past—specifically, the flirtation of its military leaders with fascism and nazism and its military and diplomatic alliance with the Germans, with all the resulting tragic consequences for Japan's neighbors and ultimately Japan itself. No process of postwar reconciliation like the one between Germany and its European neighbors has taken place in Asia. Is it that the Japanese, unlike the Germans, do not know how to apologize for deep religious, cultural, or historical reasons? Or is it somehow unrealistic and unfair for us to think about Japan in terms of analogies with Germany? For the Dutch writer Ian Buruma, it is a combination of these factors, plus another key element. Having been the first and happily so far the only victims of the atom bomb, the Japanese believe they've already paid a huge price for their wartime behavior, which they consider a mistake but not necessarily a crime. "We will be ready to apologize for starting the war in Asia when America is ready to apologize for Hiroshima," a former Japanese diplomat told me during my last visit to Japan in October 2008.

There may also be a still deeper cultural phenomenon at work. Relation to the past is one of the keys to the future, and history, it seems, is perceived differently in Europe and Asia. In a continent where the belief in reincarnation does exist, the rebuilt version of the Golden Pavilion in Kyoto burned to ashes so many times is considered as authentic as the original building. Could this "relativity" of Asian history help explain their different attitude to the past?

Most Europeans, the people of the Balkans being a major exception, have managed to transcend their past and engaged successfully in the construction of the European Union. By contrast, most Asians still have difficulty dealing with their past, and they have done so in the most selective and often contradictory manner. The Chinese, for example, take every opportunity to mention Japanese war crimes but choose to ignore their own domestic misdeeds, from the Tiananmen repression of 1989 to their recent repression of Tibet.

Even when it comes to the contrasting emotions of hope and fear, a gulf seems to separate Japan from both its neighbors in Asia and its counterparts in the West.

Japanese national fears have been traditionally very different from Western fears. Japanese fears are dominated by nature. Fear of earthquakes, tsunamis, and flooding lead Japanese families to keep survival kits at hand in the entrances of their houses. European fears, by contrast, focus on what other men can do through aggression or invasion. In a sense, the Japanese preoccupation with nature can be seen as uniquely modern in that it predates the current Western worries about the environment. But even here the difference is more significant than the similarity, for whereas the Western world focuses on what man can do to nature, the reverse is true in Japan.

However, the current culture of fear in Japan is not solely focused on natural disasters. It explains why Japan is not part of the Asian culture of hope and why today's Japanese are more in tune with the Western culture of fear. The Japanese climate of self-doubt is now nearly twenty years old, having originated in the 1988–1990 financial collapse precipitated by the bursting of its housing bubble. Japan then went through a structural crisis that lasted at least until 2002 and the accession of Prime Minister Yoichi Koizumi. (As a number of economists have noted, there are disturbing parallels between the decade-long trauma suffered by Japan in the 1990s and the financial crisis that hit the United States in 2008. It remains to be seen whether American leaders will be able to avoid a prolonged period of stagnation and decline comparable to that experienced by Japan.)

Even today Japan has not yet fully recovered from the crisis of the 1990s. One senses that the country no longer knows precisely where it is going or where it belongs. It is painfully aware of the fact that India has overtaken it as America's main diplomatic partner in Asia and that China has become America's main economic partner and global rival. In fact one senses in foreign policy circles in Tokyo and particularly in the Gaimucho, or Foreign Ministry, something like an obsession with China. It reflects the painful sense of a reduced international status from the years, prior to the 1990s, when Japan was the only important Asian country on the world stage.

But Japan's self-doubt has other root causes. Its aging population is about to become the oldest in the world, making it difficult for Japan to behave with the dynamism and energy that a culture of hope demands. Its suicide rate, especially among young people, is one of the highest in the world. And with the notable exception of the Koizumi years, the Japanese political system has been marked by what could best be described as mediocrity and stagnation. The Japanese themselves in the 1990s used to describe their system as combining the worst features of Mexico and Italy: rigidity and inefficiency.

Japan in fact shares many of the strengths and weaknesses of Europe. Both possess strong and dynamic enterprises, stable democratic systems, and high-quality health systems. But both also share a tendency to depression, introspection, anxiety, and self-absorption. Perhaps it's not surprising that the Western culture of fear should have infected Japan as well.

Diplomatically as well as emotionally, Japan is generally aligned with the West rather than with its Asian neighbors. Like such Western nations as Australia, Canada, and Germany, Japan is democratic, prosperous, a nonnuclear power, and a nonpermanent member of the United Nations Security Council. Japan tends to be "passionately moderate" in its approach to the world and often seeks to serve as a bridge across various kinds of divides: the former geographic divide between Eastern and Western Europe, the social and ethical divide between Canada and the United States (the former widely viewed as peace-loving, the latter as bellicose), the economic divide between the global north and the south, but above all the cultural divide between the East and the West. Often seen as Western in Asian eyes and Eastern in the eyes of Europeans and Americans, Japan seems to enjoy being in a kind of bridging posture.

But the ascendancy of China and India is now leaving Japan feeling less like a bridge between cultures and more like a mongrel that has been left behind, its uniqueness, importance, and influence diminished. During the decades of Japan's postwar rebuilding, generations of Japanese made economic sacrifices for the greatness and prosperity of their country, and as a nation Japan was a willing and eager student of Western-style democracy and capitalism. Now those sacrifices and those years of student status appear almost pointless as Japan's giant neighbors gather more and more power and clout without making comparable sacrifices. It is as if after being the best pupil in the class for decades, Japan is watching "bad" students being rewarded with better grades. And as China becomes an increasingly important economic partner of Japan, many Japanese are beginning to resent the fact that they are working so hard, not for the "King of Prussia" (as eighteenth-century Frenchmen used to complain) but for the "Emperor of China."

For all these reasons, Japan is now dominated by a vague sense of anxiety about its future. The hope that ruled Japan in the 1960s and 1970s has given way to fear.

THE CHALLENGES OF HOPE

In spite of their differing political systems, China and India, those two great empires of hope, are faced with remarkably similar challenges. Both countries must lift hundreds of millions of people out of absolute poverty, forestall potential ecological tragedies, prevent the further spread of the HIV-AIDS epidemic, and reduce the gap between society and politics. This last challenge, which is proving difficult even for the "mature" Western democracies, is an especially daunting task for a disorderly democracy like India and a stultified autocracy like China. The culture of hope that inspires millions of Indians and Chinese exists, for the most part, not because of their political leaders but in spite of them.

As China and India come of age on the world stage, both countries face enormous questions on their future relations with each other and with the other great powers. For each, one major challenge will be deciding how to negotiate their relationship with the United States, which remains, after all, the single greatest global power.

India has already begun taking steps to demonstrate its independence from its erstwhile American sponsors—for example, by developing plans for building an oil and gas pipeline to Iran and by pushing back against U.S. demands in the ongoing bilateral negotiations over India's civilian nuclear industry.

Today India must decide what kind of power it wants to be. Upon its birth in 1947, India viewed itself much as the European Union views itself today, as a "moral superpower," largely on the basis of its success in achieving independence peacefully under the spiritual leadership of Gandhi. But in the twenty-first century India can't rely on any nostalgia for its onetime moral status. Its key challenge in the years to come will turn on its ability to forge an international identity in relation to the United States in a mature and balanced way, dominated neither by an Indian variant of Gaullism (the quest for independence at all costs) nor by a strict balance of power view in which India's main function is to balance China on behalf of America.

Meanwhile China's power dilemma is almost the reverse of India's. One senior Western diplomat quoted by the *Financial Times* remarked, "The idea that the Chinese leadership wakes up every morning with ideas about dominating the world simply does not stand up. If anything, they wake up worrying about how to deal with a hundred different problems at home." This is right—for now. But how long will the Chinese stick to their policy of not rocking the boat? Either excessive confidence and global hubris (perhaps unlikely) or loss of confidence and the need to divert attention from domestic problems (more likely) could lead China toward some form of irresponsible nationalism, involving aggressive steps toward Taiwan, for example.

The evolution of the international roles played by China and India will depend upon the ability of the two countries to reform themselves. Can China remain an engine of growth for the global economy and become the largest trading nation in the world without accelerating the internal evolution of its policies? Will China continue to be the world's most promising new market for multinational corporations if Beijing's governance remains stultified? How will India develop a mass-scale, labor-intensive manufacturing sector without providing a minimum level of education to the millions of rural Indians now living in near-total poverty? And how long will India remain an attractive supplier of goods and services to Western companies without dramatically reducing its excessive levels of private and governmental corruption?

These challenges are real. Yet they do not weaken the case for calling Asia the continent of hope. We might even say that Chindia constitutes a reassuring basis for global hope precisely because its leaders do not see themselves as having a mission to save the world from the forces of evil (as George Bush once did) or even to set universal ethical, social, and cultural norms (as Europe sometimes does). Yet as China and India keep growing, they will have to accept the fact that responsibility comes with power and that in an interdependent world, respect for international rules and norms is part of that responsibility. It remains to be seen what the full impact of the 2008–2009 economic crisis on the two Asian giants will be. Because they are more accustomed to suffering than Westerners, and because their appetite for success is greater than ours, Asians have an ability to rebound that should not be underestimated, as they demonstrated in 1998–1999 during their first financial crisis.

From the second half of the twentieth century until today, Asia has moved from being a continent of wars to a continent of hope—even if we acknowledge that it is a modest form of hope, one based not on grand dreams of world peace and freedom but simply on a vision of steadily rising material prosperity. For the world's billions of hungry people, such a modest vision is surely an attractive one, but will it be enough in the long run? This is one of the great questions that the twenty-first century will answer.

Chapter Three

THE CULTURE OF HUMILIATION

On the existential plain, Bin Laden was marginalized, out of play, but inside the chrysalis of myth
that he had spun about himself he was becoming
a representative of all persecuted and humiliated
Muslims. His life and the symbols in which he
cloaked himself powerfully embodied the pervasive sense of dispossession that characterized the
modern Muslim world. In his own miserable exile,
he absorbed the misery of his fellow believers, his
loss entitled him to speak for theirs, his vengeance
would sanctify their suffering.
—LAWRENCE WRIGHT, THE LOOMING TOWER

If hope is confidence, humiliation is impotence, an emotion
that stems above all from the feeling that you are no longer
in control of your life either collectively, as a people, a nation,
or a religious community, or individually, as a single person.
Humiliation peaks when you are convinced that the Other has
intruded into the private realm of your own life and made you
utterly dependent. Humiliation encapsulates a sense of dispossession toward the present and even more so toward the future,

a future in utter contrast with an idealized, glorified past, a future in which your political, economic, social, cultural conditions are dictated by the Other.

Humiliation exists to some degree among all cultures and societies. Like cholesterol, it takes both good and bad forms. A certain degree of humiliation can constitute an incentive to social climbing through hard work: "I shall prove to you what I am really capable of." "I'll show you how wrong you've been not to take me seriously." "I will triumph on behalf of my disrespected and dispossessed forebears."

It can be argued that the first Asian economic miracle in the 1980s was at least in part a victorious response to national feelings of humiliation. Countries such as South Korea and even Taiwan wanted to prove to Japan, their former occupying power, that they too could perform well on the global economic stage. A similar feeling of defiance has also been one of the motors of the current Chinese renaissance. Thus the humiliation inflicted by the Japanese on the rest of Asia has constituted an energizing drug for the entire region. In turn the Japanese themselves are now exhibiting their own feelings of relative humiliation toward China. A Japanese friend has told me how good it is for the Japanese to have the Chinese as neighbors. "Without them, we would become lazy," was her comment. (But of course this observation doesn't altogether eliminate the bitterness of feeling relegated to second rank.)

When it is transcended and mastered, humiliation acts on nations as it does on individuals. It reinforces the instinct of competition. It gives energy and whets the appetite. But this presupposes the existence of a perceived or real window of opportunity, a glimmer of hope. In other words, for humiliation to be "good humiliation" requires a minimum of confidence and favorable circumstances, such as a reasonably promising political and economic context and national leadership that is up to the task of rallying a downhearted people.

By contrast, humiliation without hope leads to despair and to the nurturing of a yearning for revenge that can easily turn into an impulse toward destruction. If you cannot reach the level of those you feel are humiliating you, at least you can drag them down to your level: "I'll teach them what suffering is like."

Today this culture of "bad humiliation" is most present in large portions of the Arab-Islamic world, with the significant exception of the Gulf emirates, tiny city-states that are, at least at present, the proverbial exception that proves (i.e., tests) the rule.

First, a few words of definition.

One cannot accurately speak of Islam as a single entity. Islam has exploded into multiple incarnations that include diverse religious, cultural, national, and political variations: Shiites versus Sunnis, Arabs versus non-Arabs, Asians versus Middle Easterners, Africans versus Europeans, moderates versus radicals, religious versus agnostics. In this chapter, I try to be explicit about which threads of Islam I am alluding to at any particular moment.

Furthermore, the "Arab world" does not really exist as such. It is composed of various, highly diverse nations united by a common sense of insecurity. But if there is no Arab unity, no Arab diplomacy, no coordinated expression of Arab interest or unity, and if even the Arab League is a beleaguered multilateral institution, all of which is true, nonetheless, there is something like an "Arab emotion," a sense of Arab identity, however vague, that distinguishes Arabs from non-Arabs and in fact sets the two groups strongly at odds with each other. Not so long ago, in the postwar era, when pan-Arab nationalist dreams underpinned a clear political agenda for postcolonial leadership, this Arab emotion could be seen as a major force in world affairs. Today it has receded, giving precedence to a Muslim over an Arab identity, particularly in its opposition to the Western world.

What are the sources and meanings of this newly resurgent Muslim identity? They run deep in world history. Islam is a religious movement that appeared at the beginning of the seventh century on the margins of the great empires of the Byzantines and the Sassanids, which then dominated the Western world. In the name of this new religion, armies drawn from inhabitants of Arabia founded a new empire, the caliphate, which extended from Central Asia all the way to Spain. Under the Umayyad caliphs, the center of power of this empire moved from Arabia to Damascus in Syria and then to Baghdad in Iraq under the Abbasids.

Contemporaneous with these developments, the Arabic language spread and became the medium of a culture that went beyond Muslims. Arabic then became the equivalent of Latin at the time of the Roman Empire or English in today's world, a lingua franca used by Christians, Jews, and Muslims alike. In fact scholars even today cannot determine with certainty the religious affiliation of some of the scientific and philosophical writers of that period who lived, wrote, and thought in Arabic without necessarily being Muslims. Hence the title of an important historical exhibition mounted a few years ago in Cairo, "When the Sciences Spoke Arabic."

The Ottoman age from the sixteenth to the eighteenth century was the last great expression of the world of Islam, but it also marked the beginning of decline for a great civilization, symbolized by the fact that the ruling family spoke Turkish. The West was on the move, and the Ottoman Empire was on the defensive. And the political, economic, and military decline of Islam, which started in the eighteenth century, still goes on today.

Today, in demographic terms, Islam may be on the rise as a religion, en route perhaps to a world where Muslims are more numerous and represent a larger share of global population than ever. Psychologically and emotionally, however, what dominates the Muslim world is a sense of political and cultural humiliation and an exacerbated demand for dignity.

Encouraged by generations of leaders seemingly incapable of self-examination and unwilling to confront clearly their historical responsibilities, a majority within the Islamic world has taken to looking for scapegoats, "Others" who can be denounced as the guilty parties, those who have plotted against Islam, the Muslim world, and the Arab people. They denounce the United States, Israel, the Western world, and even, more generally, "Christians and Jews"—"Crusaders and Zionists," in the language of al Qaeda. Iran's president, Mahmoud Ahmadinejad, negates the very right of the state of Israel to exist, as if to say, "We have been humiliated for so long, but just wait; soon Israel will no longer be there to insult us by its very existence." And this flailing against external enemies spells popularity among many Muslims. According to a recent poll conducted by the Ibn Khaldun Center in Cairo, Ahmadinejad and Hezbollah leader Hassan Nasrallah are the two most popular foreign leaders in

overwhelmingly Sunni Egypt. Of course some Arabs are cha-
grined by the fact that their cause is defended with such brio
by leaders of a non-Arab (yet Muslim) nation—that the mantle
of Arab pride and honor has been seized by Tehran—and some
Arab moderates may even be shocked by what they rightly perceive as the vulgarity and cheap populism of those two popular
leaders. But they keep their reservations mostly to themselves,
convinced that the zeitgeist, the tide of history, is not going
their way.

The rise of radicalism in the Islamic world is both a cause
and an illustration of this phenomenon, which affects all the
currents of Islam, especially the ultrafundamentalist Wahhabi
among the Sunni and the Iranian Shiite. All Islamic countries
are affected, but some more than others. In fact it's tempting to
say that the closer the regime in power is to the United States,
the more these countries are affected by the rise of radicalism,
Egypt and Saudi Arabia being the best illustrations of this reality. But in countries such as Lebanon or even Jordan these tendencies exist, especially in Lebanon, where Hezbollah, with the
help of Iran and Syria, has become a state within a state.

One of the main characteristics of this Arab-Islamic world has
been the presence of radicalism as a permanent fixture within
it. Another has been its geographic expansion, from countries
like Algeria, Tunisia, and Morocco on the shores of the Mediterranean to the traditional Asian "Arc of Crisis" in countries like
Afghanistan and Pakistan. This geographic expansion has been
accompanied by the expansion of the culture of humiliation.
It is now ubiquitous in this very large and loose ensemble of
countries, which also includes Indonesia and Malaysia. Where
does it come from and what does it consist of?

THE ROOTS OF HUMILIATION: HISTORICAL DECLINE

The dominance of humiliation in the Arab-Islamic world has
many causes, but the first and most important is a sense of historical decline.

What drives the Islamist fantasies is fear of decay, an emotion that affects all civilizations, empires, nations, and cultures, but with varying timing and intensity. The Ottomans, for example, were obsessed with decay for the last three centuries of their history at least, and throughout the nineteenth century the Ottoman Empire was known as the "sick man of Europe." (Europeans, by contrast, are relative newcomers in the field of decline, having started to reflect upon their own decay after World War I with writers like Spengler and Toynbee. "We civilizations have learned we are mortal," wrote the French poet and philosopher Paul Valéry in 1922.)

The Islamic perception of decay, which can be traced back to the end of the seventeenth century, reached new depths in the last century. If in the seventh century Arabs were able to create a world into which other peoples were drawn, in the nineteenth and twentieth centuries they themselves were drawn into a new world created in Western Europe. It is as if the Arabs themselves had integrated the Hegelian vision of history and decided they belonged, in the words of the great historian Albert Hourani, "to a past moment in the development of human spirit, as if having fulfilled their mission of preserving Greek thought, they had handed on the torch of civilization to others." In this context, the Arab defeat in the 1967 Six-Day War was perceived not only as a military setback but more profoundly as a form of moral judgment. For the Egyptian economist Galal Amin (quoted by Hourani), the problem was that the Egyptians and other Arab peoples "had lost confidence in themselves." The problem was more cultural and moral than political or economic, as if the actual layers of historical humiliation that had accumulated since 1683 had fused into a new self laden with weakness, ineffectuality, and failure.

When the Christian West was in the midst of its Middle Ages, Islam was in the full bloom of Renaissance, in particular in places like Andalusia. It is interesting to note that Córdoba, Istanbul, and Isfahan are the three exemplary cities used in the newly built Islamic wing of London's Victoria and Albert Museum as symbols of Islamic civilization at its peak. Of the three, only one was Arab (Córdoba), and two of the three (Córdoba and Istanbul) are now essentially Western. Only the third (Isfahan, in Iran) is currently an Islamic city. (This may help explain the centrality of Iran in Arab eyes, as both a challenge and a model, and the relative success of the strategy of the present rulers of the country, in spite of their most "uncivilized," even barbarian approach to their own culture.)

In its totality, the explicit message of the Victoria and Albert's Islamic wing for a modern-day Muslim is both comforting and disturbing. It can be read as either "You were once great and may once again be great" or "The last time you were truly great was more than four centuries ago." In the great Egyptian novel *The Yacoubian Building* by Alaa Al Aswany (turned into a powerful film in 2006), one senses this nostalgia for a world of tolerance and refinement, in a corrupt, vulgar, also terribly poor and increasingly intolerant environment.

It is difficult to trace the origins of this sense of decay, first relative and then absolute. The moment the Christian West started its own Renaissance coincides with the beginning of the decline of Islam. The turning point was in 1683. Following their failure to take Vienna, the Ottomans realized that history was no longer "going their way," as they had believed after the conquest of Constantinople (the "new Rome of the East") in 1453. The failure of the Ottoman Empire to maintain a competitive edge over Christian Europe in regard to the development of military technology, especially firearms, proved to be a key element in the shift of power from Islam to the West.

By the end of the eighteenth century Napoleon Bonaparte was able to conquer Egypt easily, and the departure of the French was the result not of Islamic resistance but of victory by the British fleet under Horatio Nelson. To quote Bernard Lewis, "The dominant forces in the Islamic world were now outside forces. What shaped their lives was Western influence. What gave them choices was Western rivalries."

Ultimately, the Ottomans proved incapable of catching up with the West. By contrast, Meiji Japan at the end of the nineteenth century was sending "expert missions" to the Western world that were to play a key role in modernizing Japan. As a result, a rising Japan defeated a declining Russia in 1905. The missions sent by the Ottoman Empire on the Japanese model came too late, when the empire had become too weak and decadent to recapture its past power. Modernity came to Anatolia only with the rise of Kemal Atatürk, and even Kemalism itself, because it was too geographically limited and restricted to the former Ottoman core, failed to transcend fully the humiliation resulting from the fall of the Ottoman Empire.

The sense of historical decline at the root of the Arab-Islamic culture of humiliation has been reinforced and deepened by the cumulative impact of a succession of frustrations: the submission to Western imperialism in the nineteenth and early twentieth centuries; the disillusions of independence; the creation of the state of Israel; the failure of oil, at least initially, to serve as an economic and diplomatic weapon; and most of all, the inadequacy of their own leaders. This latter source of frustration is even deeper because no outside forces imposed it on the populations (although outside forces lately have helped maintain the status quo in countries such as Egypt and Saudi Arabia and have brought down by force in Iraq a regime resented by a majority of the people).

ISRAEL AS HUMILIATION

In these layers of humiliation, the frustration over the existence of Israel occupies a very specific place owing to a combination of historical, cultural, demographic, and religious reasons. The creation of the state of Israel in 1948 was in itself a symbolic shock for the Arab world. It was, in their eyes, the absolute proof of their own decay, of the duplicity of the West, of their inability to dictate their own history, a symbol of their impotence. To some in the West, the sense of dismay caused in the Arab world by the founding of Israel may seem disproportionate; Israel, after all, occupies such a tiny sliver of land in the midst of a vast Muslim-dominated region. But what mattered so much was not of course the size of the country but its central "emotional location," in the midst of what Arabs and Muslims considered their own lands, including Jerusalem, with its Dome of the Rock, one of the holiest sites of Islam.

The only way Arab regimes were able to come to terms with the humiliating impotence symbolized by their failure to pre-

vent or eradicate Israel has been through a mixture of historical romanticism and negation. The analogy between the newly
created Jewish state and the Crusader kingdoms of the Middle
Ages was the first psychological answer. According to this analogy, like the Christian kingdoms, Israel was a fragile and artificial creation that could never last. In reality, the analogy was
not historically strong or accurate. But this didn't deter the Arab
mythmakers. They convinced themselves that the sands of the
desert would swallow up the arrogant towers of Israel just as
they had covered the Christian castles in the past.

In 2001, before 9/11 but in the midst of the second intifada, a
high French dignitary asked a certain Saudi prince, "Why don't
you help the Palestinians financially much more than you do?
It would greatly help secure peace between Israel and Palestine."
The answer of the Saudi prince was crystal clear: "It would be
a waste of money, since Israel will not exist twenty years from
now."

Of course Saudi Arabia has profoundly changed its views after 9/11, and so have the majority of the Gulf countries, under
the dual influence of fear for the survival of their regimes if
chaos were to spread from Palestine to the Gulf and growing
economic confidence bolstered by the rise of energy prices. In
the Gulf emirates one senses also today the desire to become
the epicenter of an Islamic renaissance, which means the presence of Jews (even as Israelis) in their midst. Yet these changes
in attitude are relatively superficial compared with the abiding
desire in the hearts of millions of Muslims to see Israel removed
forever from the map of the Middle East.

Perhaps the country that felt most humiliated by the continued existence of Israel was Egypt. The Six-Day War shattered
the Arab nationalist ambitions of President Nasser. He'd successfully confronted the anachronistic neo-imperial actions of Great
Britain and France in 1956 with the help of the United States
and the Soviet Union. But now, in 1967, a country of a little
more than three million people had single-handedly destroyed
his army in one blow of aerial superiority. What was worse, that
country not only was the incarnation of Western arrogance and
superiority but also presented itself as the spiritual descendants

of the slaves of Egypt. How could a handful of former slaves so humiliate the heirs of Ramses II?

To initiate the peace process with Israel, Sadat had first to restore the damaged pride of Egyptians. The crossing of the Suez Canal in 1973 was the first step in a process that culminated symbolically with Sadat's trip to Jerusalem in 1977. Of course he paid for this daring move, so far in advance of the sensitivity of his people and of the Arab nation at large, with his life. Most Egyptians were ready for an indefinite truce or some kind of cold peace with Israel, but not for true reconciliation with Israel.

Sadat's attempt to seize hope in the midst of humiliation failed, and his death spelled an end to the effort. Under Mubarak, Egypt has been ruled by a stultified gerontocracy whose only clear priority is retaining power. A war with Israel has become impossible, but so is a true peace. Egyptians' frustrations with their own leaders have been simply too great. And of course the religious opponents of Mubarak, incarnated in the Muslim Brotherhood, have their own religious and ideological reasons to hate both the Jews and Israel.

It is only fair to say that Israelis themselves have encouraged the sense of humiliation in the Arab-Islamic world. By continuing to expand their settlements in spite of the promises made to Palestinians and to the international community, Israelis have demonstrated their careless attitude toward Palestinian sensitivities. The multiplication of controls and roadblocks within the territories controlled by Israel has played a major role in this systematic policy of humiliation that has gone beyond the requirements of security in confronting terrorism.

Of course these Israeli actions have been driven by that nation's own sense of insecurity. In the climate of hubris that followed the Six-Day War, Israel's sense of achievement and relief was mingled with a sense of superiority toward the defeated enemy. It was common in Israel in those years to hear comments such as "Israel has a secret weapon, the Arabs." Today many Arabs would be willing to bet that the Arabs have a secret weapon, the psychological fragility of Israel. Both parties are of course deeply wrong in underestimating the resilience of their adversary and overstating their own strength. In the end the burden of responsibility for the failure of the peace process must be shared among Palestinians, Israelis, Arab leaders, and the international community as a whole.

Surrounded by hostile neighbors, Israel must engage in a macabre balancing act in which quality offsets quantity, wealth balances the desperation of poverty, and technological superiority counters the passion and sacrificial spirit of the Arab masses. This balance of power game led to the second intifada (2000–2002) and the war in Lebanon (2006) and the war on Hamas in Gaza (in the winter of 2008–2009). In 2006 the lack of a clear Israeli victory spelled defeat for Israel; the lack of a clear defeat was a victory for Hezbollah. Below a ratio of one Israeli casualty for ten Arabs, Israel was "balanced." The operation in Gaza was at least in part meant to restore Israel's deterrent power and to reinstill fear in its adversaries.

In their effort to counter the sophisticated precision arsenals of Israel, the humiliated Palestinians sought to instill terror in the Israelis through the use of human bombs, intelligent weapons of destruction that could be detonated in times and places chosen to inflict maximum casualties. It was a perfectly inhuman strategy, which only toughened the resolution and character of Israeli citizens. In time it was seen as a strategic failure and a negative propaganda tool by most Palestinians themselves, but a perfect illustration of the form of violence induced by a culture of humiliation.

The political manipulation of humiliation has taken many forms, not only in the Arab-Islamic world but also in Asia. Muslims from India to Indonesia and from Malaysia to the Philippines have expressed through violence their sense of humiliation at the hands of the West—in particular, at the hands of America and of their own corrupt governments allied to the United States. The scandal surrounding the publication of caricatures of the Prophet in a Danish newspaper in 2005 is a case in point. Certainly freedom of the press should not include the right to uselessly insult the deepest emotions of others. One does not play with matches next to a gas tank; one does not deliberately attack the most sacred beliefs of the Other merely because it is a "good provocation." But it's equally obvious that the power of those cartoons to ignite fury throughout the Islamic world was due to the underlying sense of humiliation that has prepared Muslims to respond with defensive rage against any perceived insult to their own embattled faith.

Interestingly enough, the violence did not erupt among the Muslims of Denmark but in the distant capitals of an enraged Muslim world, from Karachi to Tripoli. Naturally so, for that is where the culture of humiliation exists in full force.

THE DIPLOMACY OF HUMILIATION

The sense of humiliation can sometimes be a powerful diplomatic weapon, as illustrated by a number of episodes in the recent history of the Middle East. One way it works is by playing on the sense of guilt felt by other nations that may have participated in the humiliation of your people and using this guilt to extract concessions or support.

The exploitation of the guilt feelings of former colonial powers is a classical instrument of diplomacy that Muslim countries have mastered, but this strategy tends to be eroded with the process of time. The state of Israel has not shied away from using another powerful guilt feeling of the European continent, guilt over the historical crimes of anti-Semitism and above all the Holocaust. Caught between these contradictory guilt feelings, Europe has had trouble defining a common and viable position in the region of the Middle East. Germany is tilted toward Israel, while Great Britain (with no direct Holocaust guilt) and France (perceived as a nation of anti-Nazi resistance fighters under de Gaulle, in spite of the Vichy regime) were at times poised toward the emotions of their former imperial possessions while at the same time (in the words of one American diplomat) "stooping for oil" and thereby reacting with a combination of guilt and greed.

In their unending negotiation with the West on nuclear issues, the Iranian representatives for their part have always started discussions with a reference to their former prime minister Mossadegh, who was ousted by a U.S.-led coup in 1953. Like an incantation, his name is used as a weapon of emotional deterrence: "You humiliated us more than fifty years ago, but you will not be able to repeat it today. We are a major actor now. We are as entitled to become nuclear as any country of the region. We have better qualifications as a civilization than Pakistan, and in demographic terms we are not even in the same category as tiny Israel." The strategy may not always work, but at times it serves to weaken Western resolve, and in diplomacy even small advantages can be important.

Even Turkey in its own way plays the emotional card when the external world tries to reproach it with its own past. The attempt to recognize the tragic slaughter of Armenians by Turks (1915–1919) as an act of genocide by the American Congress in 2007 only worsened a deteriorating Turkish-American relationship following the war in Iraq. Although Turks may look down upon Arabs and consider Iran a strategic threat, a sense of common Muslim humiliation nevertheless pushes them to react emotionally when they are confronted with their own past, especially by the West. "You have no lessons to give us; look what you did to your native Indians and to your Jews" seems to be the implicit motto of Ankara.

On the other hand, humiliation may sometimes be hidden for a combination of political, diplomatic, and even religious reasons.

In 1979 the decisive help of a French elite commando in the retaking of the holy sites of Mecca from a group of Islamic fundamentalists was kept secret as much as possible by the Saudi regime. The regime was afraid to reveal the entrance of "infidels" into such symbolic sanctuaries of Islam and was also reluctant to admit its own failure at facing down what was seen later as the birth of al Qaeda. The fact that Arab princes needed the West to protect their holy shrines, their personal security, and the stability of their regimes was a source of deep personal and national shame for those leaders. Even today arms sales from the West can be seen as a form of discreet cover-up for a more personalized form of protection. "We will buy your weapons systems, but the understanding is that you will protect

the integrity of our regimes with your elite troops if need be."
What kind of independence is this? Is it less humiliating to rely
on Western support than it was to rely on the Ottoman emperor
in the years before independence? At least the Ottomans were
good Muslims. . . .

Humiliation may also be hidden under a facade of intellectual arrogance, leading to the proclamation "The future belongs
to us, just as the past did!" For a Syrian philosopher quoted by
Bernard Lewis, the only remaining question about the future of
Europe is: "Will it be an Islamized Europe, or a Europeanized Islam?" Such bravado is cold comfort for the millions of Muslims
smarting under present-day humiliations that show no sign of
being alleviated in the short run.

HUMILIATION, GLOBALIZATION, AND DENIAL

Frustration with the process of globalization has been adding to
all these layers of humiliation. In our transparent and open world,
the world of Islam is painfully aware of the growing contrast
between the success of the Western and Asian worlds at surfing
on the waves of globalization and its own failure to do so. The
United Nations' Arab Human Development Report, published
in 2002, constituted a kind of wake-up call that was difficult for
Arab leaders to ignore. It contained a series of alarming statistics,
ranging from the very low level of investment in education and
research (except in the Gulf countries) to the lack of economic
competitiveness, the absence of democratic progress, and the
deepening inequality. All these data reinforced the feeling of a
"world left behind." As the noted Middle East expert Olivier Roy
has brilliantly demonstrated in his book *Globalized Islam: The Search
for a New Ummah*, the Muslim backlash against Westernization is a
logical response to the spread of Islam beyond traditional borders as well as a reaction to the sense of impotence produced by
continued failure: "I cannot and will not succeed in the world
they control and define, so I will create my own world in which
success is defined as I see fit."

Yet all this begs the question, Why this pervasive sense of

failure and impotence? Are socioeconomic problems inherent to the Muslim religion? For example, can they be traced to the fact that the Koran draws no clear division between the spiritual and worldly realms? Is Islam somehow incompatible with modernity, capitalism, and democracy? Or will democratic electoral processes, in the absence of a democratic culture and a strong middle class, inevitably elevate nondemocratic forces, as in the victory of Hamas in Palestine or the defeat of moderates in Iran?

The evidence of recent history gives little reason to be hopeful about the emergence of a modernist, democratic Islam. Even in the more modern, developed Turkey, the progress of democracy has coincided with the recent rise of Islamist parties. Many in the West were pleased by the claims of Recep Tayyip Erdoğan, head of Turkey's Justice and Development Party, that it was or would become a Muslim equivalent of the Christian Democratic Union in Germany. But the German Christian Democrats are democrats first, Christians second. Judged by the relative intolerance they demonstrate toward other political forces, many followers of Erdoğan are Muslims first, democrats second (if at all).

It seems clear that the relationship between Islam and politics is somehow fundamentally different from that between Christianity and politics. But this does not necessarily mean that democracy is an alien system to Islam. An increasing number of Muslim intellectuals in societies as diverse as Egypt, Jordan, Turkey, Iran, Malaysia, and Indonesia are now exploring (in the words of scholar James Piscatori) "how what they regard as the intrinsically Islamic values of pluralism, tolerance and civic participation can be implemented" in their countries' political cultures.

These intellectuals would not agree with the dark vision of Islam presented by the controversial Somali-born Dutch feminist writer Ayaan Hirsi Ali. For Ali in her challenging essay *The Caged Virgin*, the problems are inherent to Islam itself. In her words, a "Muslim's relationship with his God is one of fear." The second element of the problem, she claims, is that Islam knows only one moral source, the infallible Prophet Muhammad. And "[t]he third element is that Islam is strongly dominated by a sexual morality derived from tribal Arab values dating from the time the Prophet received his instructions from Allah." (For this reason, the presence of women soldiers in the American army stationed on Islamic land must inevitably be perceived as a particularly aggressive form of humiliation.) For Ali, "these elements explain largely why Muslim nations are lagging behind the West and more recently, also lagging behind Asia."

What is certain is that the nonintegration of women as equal actors in the functioning of society constitutes a profound, though unacknowledged, handicap for a majority of Islamic countries attempting to compete in a globalized world. I vividly recall a lecture I gave in Berlin just a few days after 9/11 to an audience of investment bankers from the Gulf emirates, including top executive women, each clad in an impeccable business suit and adorned with a light veil. These women were offended by my remarks on Islam's treatment of women and set about trying to convince me that their positions as women in their respective financial institutions could not be matched by those of Western women. They were in denial of a reality that they deemed humiliating. If a woman cannot drive her own car in a country like Saudi Arabia, how can she play a significant autonomous role in society?

Similarly, when President Ahmadinejad was the guest of Columbia University in his trip to attend the United Nations General Assembly in September 2007, he emphasized, against all evidence, that the condition of women in Iran "was the best in the world." (He also declared that there were no homosexuals in Iran, raising the question why it would be necessary to prescribe hanging as the punishment for a crime that evidently does not exist.)

Perhaps it's not surprising that a culture laboring under a burden of humiliation should find it unbearably painful to acknowledge that fact and that one of the strategies it employs to master this discomfort is simple denial, even of the obvious.

ISLAM AND CHRISTIANITY

The relationship between Islam and Christianity constitutes an important element in the building up of this culture of humiliation. They are the two monotheistic faiths that perceive themselves as universal, exclusive, and intent on converting others. Thus the growth of the West—whether in its Christian/ capitalist form or its later Marxist/atheist incarnation—could only be perceived in the lands of Islam as the pursuit of their malediction. The spread of Western culture and faith into countries once held by Islam meant that once again Muslims were not in control of their faith and history.

The religious competition between Islam and Christianity has taken new shapes recently. First, whereas Islam is now an expanding religion booming with energy, Christianity is to a large extent, especially in Europe, a retreating one. Even if one does not fully accept Walter Laqueur's description of Europe as "the continent where the churches are empty and the mosques full," one must acknowledge that Christian religious practices are in decline across the continent. Vocations to the priesthood are shrinking to an alarmingly low level; there are now more Jesuits in Asia than in Europe. By contrast, the number of Islamic worshippers around the world, including North America and Europe, has been growing steadily. Yet because this rise of Islam is not accompanied by any noticeable economic, social, or political progress, its growing popularity as a religion does not serve to assuage the sense of humiliation among Muslims. And all too often, Islam's role in the lives of Muslims is simply as a set of rules, restrictions, and rituals rather than as a practical enhancement of ordinary existence. In the madrassas of Pakistan, youths memorize the Koran in Arabic, a language they do not understand. Under such circumstances, religion can hardly be connected in any positive way with the improvement of daily life.

Between the rising relevance of religion in an environment obsessed with its own sense of decline and the growing indifference to religion in a culture that still perceives itself as universal and central, the relationship can only be difficult. "We" in the West are increasingly secular. "They" in the Islamic world are increasingly religious. As a result, "we" may see "them" as an anachronistic evocation of "our" past, between the sixteenth and seventeenth centuries, when Europe was in the midst of religious wars. What "they" perceive, by contrast, is that because of our modernity (which they perceive as moral decadence), they are no longer in control of their private lives. "Our" casual approach to sexuality signals that they are no longer in charge of their values, that we despise or ignore their sensitivities.

Of course many progressive Muslims, both in the West and in the rest of the world, are bent on destroying this "we" versus "they" dichotomy. A growing number of well-educated second-generation Muslim women in Europe, America, and Islamic nations are choosing to fight for women's rights from within Islam. This may be, in time, the most powerful revolution of all. And of course, in a world of global communications networks, no culture is immune to cross-border influences. In a recently published book, *Heavy Metal Islam: Rock, Resistance, and the Struggle for the Soul of Islam,* writer Mark LeVine examines Western-influenced underground music movements that have blossomed under authoritarian regimes across the Middle East and North Africa. But while LeVine's purpose may be to shatter the notion of irreconcilable differences between Islam and the West, mainstream Muslims may take from it just the opposite lesson: "See how the West is corrupting our youths with its decadent music! We need to erect stronger barriers against such evils."

The issue of polygamy is a perfect illustration of the gulf in perceptions that exists between traditional Islam and the West. To the Western mind, it is an offense to modernity and to the rights of women. But to a devout Muslim, it is a perfect accomplishment of the laws of Islam. Our condemnation reminds some Muslims of a harsh reality: that they are now living under "our" international and national laws. And it should be so when Muslims live as members of a minority in the Western world. There is a fine line between the need to respect the values of others and the danger of extreme cultural relativism, which abandons all rules and standards in the name of universal acceptance.

This question of tolerance is yet another sore point between Muslims and Christians. Some Muslims want to claim that in fact Islam is the most tolerant of the great monotheistic faiths. They point to historical circumstances in which Jews and Christians as minorities in the land of Islam were treated with benevolence. There's some truth to this: In the eighteenth century Voltaire, in his denunciation of Christian intolerance, noted that churches could be found in Islamic countries while mosques were never seen in Christian countries. But Islamic tolerance for other faiths has varied over time, being greater when confidence has prevailed over self-doubt. Today the reverse of Voltaire's observation is closer to the truth. There are mosques in the Christian West, even in Rome, but no churches in Saudi Arabia. Our modern multiculturalist attempts at "constructive engagement" with Islam do not necessarily satisfy or appease hard-liners in the Muslim world, who perceive them as signs of hypocrisy or weakness. As for mainstream Muslims, they want respect when we are ready to give them merely tolerance.

ARAB CULTURAL DECLINE

The mostly political and social sources of humiliation are reinforced at a cultural level with the decline of the Arab language and culture. While Islam as a religion may be expanding, Arab culture is not thriving. With a few notable exceptions, such as the Egyptian novelist and Nobel laureate Naguib Mahfouz and his countryman the playwright Kateb Yacine, Arab literature, music, and movies have little currency outside their homelands. At the same time, the flow of Western literature into the Arab world via translations into Arabic, while evidently increasing in recent years, is still weak, a reflection of the relative isolation of the Arab world from global culture. Even within the Islamic world, contemporary culture finds little encouragement—often the reverse. It is dangerous to be an intellectual or an artist in an environment where despots and fundamentalists have a shared interest in curbing the free expression of creativity. Thus Algerian Kabyle singer Lounès Matoub was assassinated in 1998 for the "crime" of advocating freedom for the Berbers, as well as for the "sacrilegious" lyrics of his songs.

Of course great differences exist among Muslim countries. Nothing is more striking from this standpoint than the contrast between bookshops in Cairo and those in Istanbul. The former merely illustrate the provincialism of a decaying gerontocratic state, while the latter are booming with life. The Turkish Nobel prizewinner Orhan Pamuk may be a kind of dissident in his own country, but he is surely not a fluke. In many ways, Pamuk is the symbolic illustration of the fact that the decline we are describing is affecting much more the Arab world than the Islamic world.

Egypt once saw itself as the proud inheritor of a great pre-Islamic culture. The physical continuity between modern and ancient Egypt is much more real than the continuity between modern-day Greece and classical Greece. I remember vividly how struck I was more than twenty years ago, when after having met the foreign minister of Egypt Neguib, I could see his physical ancestor in the Egyptian Museum of Antiquities: The famous sculpture of the "scribe" looked just like him. Egypt then could still perceive itself as its own sort of Middle Empire, the indispensable actor and the equivalent for the Middle East of what China was for Asia.

This is no longer the case. Frozen by a regime that has achieved too little and lasted too long, Egypt has lost the sense of confidence that its memories of the age of the pharaohs had given it. In this sense, it summarizes and incarnates perfectly what has gone wrong with the Arab world.

I still remember the posters I saw on the walls of Cairo in 1986 on the eve of presidential elections that would once again confirm the presidency of Hosni Mubarak. Portraits of Nasser were followed by portraits of Sadat and huge Rothko-like green posters representing a new wave of Egyptian politics, the Muslim Brotherhood. The message was clear: "Egyptians, you have tried Arab nationalism with Nasser and Egyptian nationalism with Sadat. Both failed. Why not try the party of God, the Muslim Brotherhood?" The Muslim Brothers today are used by the regime—at least in part—to frighten both domestic and foreign audiences into accepting the political status quo: "Do you think we're bad? We're better than the alternative!"

God as the response to failure, God as the ultimate solution: This is the path that too many in the Islamic world have chosen, a path that is ultimately futile because it offers no meaningful way to address the challenges of modernity, challenges to which every nation on earth must somehow respond.

HUMILIATION AND TERRORISM

Many in the West have expressed bafflement over the fact that Islamist views, including extreme views advocating violence, have found sympathetic ears not only among the poor and dispossessed in Arab and Muslim countries but even among those of relatively high social, economic, and educational status. Like the revolutionaries of nineteenth-century Europe, the terrorists of the twenty-first century are not recruited among the poorest. In fact their level of affluence and education is usually average, if not above average. The reason is simple: The culture of humiliation has affected all levels of Islamic society, from the poorest to the most affluent and Westernized.

Consider, as an example, the life and career of the great scholar Edward Said, author of the famous 1978 essay *Orientalism*. That book is, at least in part, a product of the sense of humiliation and alienation that even a highly assimilated Christian Arab could feel. If the most sophisticated of literary critics and a refined amateur pianist could denounce with such passion the "arrogant" way in which the West was looking at the "Orient," all classes of society could be united by such an emotion. And who can fully condemn Edward Said? There is obviously an element of truth in what he felt and wrote.

The same culture of humiliation underlies the attraction of many Muslims to terrorist violence. Without the culture of humiliation, how could fundamentalists manage to push a young educated Muslim Briton to kill fellow Britons in a suicide attack on the London tube? How could young Germans converted to Islam plot murderous attacks on their own country? These self-destructive instincts are brought to life by a combination of psychological, cultural, and socioeconomic conditions that lead from humiliation to violence.

In a recently released report titled "Radicalization in the Western World: The Domestic Threat," the New York Police Department describes the process through which an autonomous jihad, neither guided, controlled, nor financed by al Qaeda but certainly inspired by it, has been formed in the West. The conclusion of this report is that the search for identity and the failure of social and economic integration is playing a greater role than oppression, despair, or the spirit of revenge as incubators of radicalization. These negative emotions can easily lead to belief in conspiracy theories and a willingness to turn to violence as a source of redemption.

The sense that the Islamic world is under assault in geopolitical terms has played a crucial role in the rise of modern Muslim fundamentalism and the terrorism it fosters. Consider, for example, the Soviet invasion of Afghanistan. It was a symbolic emotional turning point after the peak of Arab humiliation in the Six-Day War of 1967. The Islamists rallied to support the Afghan rebels against the Soviets (with clandestine help from the other superpower, the United States). The unexpected success of the rebels provided proof that a superpower, if a decaying one, could be defeated by an Islamic national upsurge.

Of course defeating the Soviet Union in Afghanistan was not enough to alleviate the Islamic sense of humiliation, for the true "humiliators," in the view of most Muslims, were in the West. It merely reinforced the appetite for revenge of the fundamentalists, with results that played out on 9/11 and continue to affect world events to this day.

The deepening of the Israel-Palestine conflict also played a role in encouraging terrorism. For one thing, it inhibited condemnation of terrorism among Arabs and Muslims. True, there were innocent victims of terror attacks, but what about the sufferings of the Palestinians and the injustice done to them? At least the terrorists were—in a negative way, of course—redressing the legitimate grievances of the Arab and Muslim peoples. Today this perception is slowly changing, as the main victims of Islamic terrorism are now Muslims, as in a country like Iraq, for example.

I've had firsthand experience of the spread of conspiracy theories encouraged by the culture of humiliation. In the months that followed 9/11, many of my cabdrivers of North African origins in Paris were convinced that Israeli agents from the Mossad had been responsible for the attacks in New York. I wondered why. Did they assume that Arabs unaided were incapable of such a feat? It was of course an absurd theory, but they believed it, perhaps as a way of resolving their own internal conflict between the pride and guilt they felt about the actions of al Qaeda. (The Pakistani-born writer Mohsin Hamid has well expressed this duality of emotions in his novel *The Reluctant Fundamentalist*.)

MUSLIMS IN THE WEST

For most Arabs and Muslims living in Western countries, the sense of humiliation and frustration they feel is as much cultural as socioeconomic in nature. What leads them to despair is their deep feeling of alienation from most of the modern world, a frustration that is all the more painful because of the scars from a not so distant colonial past. Where this colonial history has particular resonance, the sense of alienation is particularly profound. For example, in 2001, French citizens of Algerian descent booed their national team (that is, the French team), while in 2008, Germans of Turkish descent happily cheered both the German and Turkish teams. The reason is simple: There is no colonial legacy between Germany and Turkey, whereas Algeria and France share a difficult history that neither country finds easy to forget.

But even in the absence of a colonial history, Muslims in the West are often cut off from their communities, especially in times of conflict. After the Gulf War in 1991, Arabs felt excluded from the Western world (as if, in Western eyes, all Arabs from Iraq to Algeria were alike). After 9/11, Muslims felt excluded from the world at large (as if all Muslims were potential terrorists). And following the explosion of violence in French cities in 2005, French Muslims felt excluded as *banlieusards* in their own country (as if all Muslims were inhabitants of poor and dangerous suburban slums).

Undoubtedly European Muslims suffer from political, social, sexual, and urban segregation. Politically they are treated as suspicious because of their culture and religion, socially because of their names and their addresses. They have trouble finding jobs (their unemployment rate is three times as high as that among

nonimmigrants). They get into trouble with the law (representing just 15 percent of the French urban population, they are 70
to 80 percent of those incarcerated). They have difficulty finding
romantic partners; who wants to fall in love with a young man
without a future from a culture that tends to oppress women?
And they tend to live in semiurban ghettos, so close and yet
so far from the cities whose lights, dynamism, and splendor
contrast painfully with their daily lives. And so during the riots
of November 2005, French Muslims burned schools (republican symbols of a social mobility that excluded them) and cars
(capitalist symbols of a physical mobility they could not enjoy).
In the aftermath, polls showed that the level of negative attitude
toward migrants had increased dramatically (rising from 38 to
56 percent in one year).

I was invited recently to a naturalization ceremony by a
friend of mine who had just become eligible for French citizenship. Although it was a cold, rainy day, the citizens-to-be
had to wait outside the annex of the Paris prefecture where the
ceremony was to take place and were told in curt and unpleas-
ant tones to queue "properly" by the police officer in charge. It
was a test of strength and will to get through the narrow door;
the atmosphere was one of confusion, if not hostility; and in
the end accompanying friends and family were not allowed to
enter. One could sense open suspicion in the body language
of the security guards, as if to say, "You are about to become
French, but do you deserve the honor?" Where were the values
of the republic, especially the "fraternity" of which we boast?
I could only compare this first harsh greeting with the solemn,
quasireligious naturalization ceremonies in the United States. I
felt ashamed of my country.

For Muslims in Europe, humiliation comes above all from
a difficult search for identity. The difficulty of integration into
French society, combined with alienation from the countries
of their roots (Algeria, Morocco, Tunisia), makes them too often orphans with no national identity. In the three countries
of North Africa that came under the control of France's "mission to civilize"—in particular in Algeria, which was legally a
full-fledged part of France—children were actually taught that
their ancestors were *les gaulois* and thus were dispossessed of a

history they had no means of knowing. But they were treated not as "real" French citizens but as *indigènes*, good enough for military service but not for full citizenship. They could die as French but not live that way.

Over time the situation has improved. A few rare individuals have achieved notable success in European society. But there are still no significant French, German, or British cultural, social, and political leaders who come from the Muslim communities of those countries.

In this context, Islam becomes a young person's primary identity: "If I am not yet French and I am no longer an Algerian, who am I if not a Muslim?"

In Great Britain citizens of Pakistani descent suffer from the same identity angst, reinforced by the fact that Pakistan's sense of national identity is at best problematic. What is the meaning of a concept such as an Islamic nation? Is Islam, in this case, a culture, a nationality, or a religion? And what makes Pakistan "Islamic" more than any other nation? There are more Muslims living in neighboring India than there are in Pakistan. Is Pakistan an artificial construction, an arbitrary outgrowth of history that has failed to turn into a nation? If so, what does that do to the sense of self and of connection to a people that human beings need to feel completely secure?

At the same time, other, less lofty factors seem to play a crucial role in nurturing the feeling of humiliation. In "My Brother the Bomber," a fascinating study of one of the terrorists of the 7/7 attacks on London, the roots of violence are traced primarily to family feuds and tensions among British Pakistanis of various generations. The younger generation are said to view Islamism—in this case, Wahhabi fundamentalism—as a kind of liberation theology. Caught in intractable identity dilemmas of a religious, sexual, and family nature, these young men were an easy prey to the seductions of religious extremists, who gave a meaning to their alienated and lonely lives through destruction and death, including their own.

Again, the sense of Arab-Islamic humiliation fostered by a life of poverty and isolation in the modern world feeds and is fed by a sense of historical decline. The more you believe that you and your civilization were once the center of the world, the greater the sense of humiliation you feel over your current degraded state. Thus the glorious past is not comforting but rather a deep source of frustration, at least for Arabs and Muslims who are aware of and preoccupied by the notion of an ancient golden age of Islamic civilization.

This describes a minority of Arabs and Muslims undoubtedly. Few young Muslims in the suburbs of French cities are motivated by any nostalgia for past Arab glory when they start burning cars. Nor are they motivated primarily by current political issues, such as the Palestinian-Israeli conflict. For the typical young Muslim, the Middle East conflict is far away and deeply confusing (which should they side with, Hamas or Fatah?).

Nonetheless, geopolitical fantasies of ancient glory, and perhaps of a future restoration, are clearly part of today's culture of humiliation. Extremist fundamentalists dream of restoring the greatness of the caliphate, of Reconquista, the restoration of Muslim control over the vast empire once controlled by Islam, from the Strait of Gibraltar to the banks of the Indus. And although only a few of their fellow Muslims take them seriously, their declarations encourage the Cassandras of the Western world, particularly those who predict that Europe is condemned to become an Islamicized "Eurabia." Thus the extremists excacerbate fears, tensions, and suspicions on both sides, even beyond what their numbers would seem to justify.

WHAT IS TO BE DONE?

The Islamic culture of humiliation to which the West has contributed creates various dilemmas for Western leaders.

One is the question of Samuel Huntington's clash of civilizations theory. Is there something inherent in Islamic and Christian cultures that makes conflict between them inevitable? If one emphasizes the emotional dimensions of the problem, as we do in this essay, it becomes apparent that certain distinctions need to be drawn immediately.

The first distinction to be made is between the Arab and the Islamic world. If the expression "culture of humiliation" has any meaning, it applies above all to the Arab world. It is there that the heart of the problem and the maximum of humiliation are present. However, it is now extremely difficult to separate the Arab world from the world of Islam. For what is Islam without the Arabs, Arab language, Arab culture, and Arab civilization? Although many Arabs in their quest for a meaningful identity and role in relation to a rapidly changing, hostile-seeming outside world may take refuge in the fact that they are Muslims, it is difficult for Muslims not to be embroiled by Arab emotions.

This interweaving of Arab emotions and the culture of humiliation helps explain the lack of popular mobilization in the broader Islamic world against the most unacceptable words and deeds of the Islamist fundamentalists. "Not in our name" demonstrations did indeed take place in the Islamic world expressing antiterrorist sentiments after 9/11, but they were the exception more than the rule.

Of course the relative weakness of the antiviolence mobilization within Islam has many causes. The lack of a clear organization and clear representative leaders within the Muslim communities, especially in the Western world, not to mention the deep divisions within Islam, did contribute to the relative apathy among moderate Muslims. But there was more than that. There was the sense that while the 9/11 attacks were reprehensible and would probably have negative consequences for Muslim communities all over the world, they were nonetheless understandable. America's arrogance had to be punished.

Muslims weren't the only ones to entertain such thoughts, of course. Some intellectuals, like Jean Baudrillard in France, expressed similar feelings in their writings after 9/11. And no simplification is more flawed—or dangerous—than the equation of Islam or even of Islamists with terrorism. Such an identification plays into the hands of those Islamists who argue loudly that the phrase "war on terror" is just a Western euphemism for what is really a "war on Islam."

It is also clear that when one speaks of the link between religion and terrorism, one should go beyond Islam. It was Yigal Amir, an ultrareligious Jew, who assassinated Yitzhak Rabin in 1995 "on orders from God." Terrorism has been used equally by Catholics and Protestants in the violent course of recent Irish history. The Spanish government first suspected the ETA Basque terrorist group after the Madrid bombings in March 2005.

Nonetheless, so many Muslims have now become so deeply identified with the Arab culture of humiliation that anti-Western terrorism has found at least some degree of sympathy throughout the Islamic world.

At the same time, for the West to cover all terrorists (let alone all terrorist sympathizers) with the same blanket would be a terrible mistake. Terrorists are extremely diverse in their identities and in their objectives. The declaration of global war on terrorism that followed 9/11 may have been emotionally understandable from an American point of view. But it was a policy doomed to fail. Despite Philip Bobbitt's contention in his latest book, *Terror and Consent: The Wars for the Twenty-first Century*, terrorism is not an enemy that can be vanquished. It is a violent tactic that will continue to be used as long as it is deemed effective.

Nonetheless, for the West to manage the terrorism problem and reduce it to a level at which it poses an acceptable threat should be entirely possible. Only a few hundred terrorists are considered dangerous in countries like France and Germany (which have, respectively, more than five and three million Muslims). And terrorism uses up its practitioners rather quickly. Lenin used to say, "You cannot be a revolutionary all your life," and the same is true of terrorists (even aside from the fact that the life of a terrorist tends to be short). And though the "war on terror" can never be won (in the sense of eradicating terrorism completely, once and for all), terrorists also never win. Only their targets can defeat themselves, by losing faith in their cause or by violating the values they stand for in their fight against terror. This is a crucial reality that every Western leader must remember and that Western citizens must bear in mind when demagogues exaggerate the terrorist threat for political reasons.

The Arab-Islamic culture of humiliation has other important implications beyond its role in fostering terrorism. As I've already noted, many Arabs have mixed feelings about Iran. Although they may feel threatened by its present growth, they admire the radicalism of a country that dares confront the West and its creation, Israel, in the most forceful way. The present leadership in Tehran basks in this emotional reality. Hossein

Shariatmadari, the editor of the leading Persian newspaper in Iran, the conservative *Kayhan Daily*, and an influential promoter of the Islamic revolution, observes, "The Iranian people feel they have dignity and the era of being bullied is over," and he adds, "If Tehran interferes in Arab issues such as in Palestine and Lebanon, it is because people there are defending the Islamic world and identity, and that leaves Iran no choice but to support them."

Some in the Arab world are deeply aware of the problems that the culture of humiliation has caused. In *Being Arab*, the last book he published before being assassinated by a Beirut car bomb explosion at the hands of assailants still unknown, Samir Kassir, the best-known columnist of the Lebanese daily newspaper *An Nahar*, spoke of "the Arab malaise." The worst aspect of this malaise, Kassir wrote, was the refusal of Arabs to emerge from it. He added that for him, the power of attraction of jihadist Islamism resided in the fact that it is "only ideology that seems to offer relief from the victim status the Arabs delight in claiming."

The culture of death, Kassir observed, is part of that deep malaise. If victory cannot be attained, "bloodletting others may at least be a consolation." This vendetta-like logic has reached a new peak in the last decade: "[D]eath has become the indispensable means to a desired end, if not an actual end in itself."

The only solution, Kassir wrote, is a change in attitude. The Arab world must put "victimhood" into perspective. "We must replace Arabs' customary assumption of victim status not by cultivating a logic of power or a spirit of revenge, but by recognizing the fact that, despite bringing defeats, the twentieth century has also brought benefits that can enable Arabs to participate in progress."

From that standpoint, progress is still a long way off. The status of women is one crucial reason. Across the population of the twenty-two members of the Arab League, in spite of the fact that adult literacy has doubled and women's literacy has tripled over the past thirty years, women's illiteracy remains at 60 percent. Women are the vehicle for progress and modernity in developing societies. Women are not only biologically the vehicle for the future, but the instrument of hope, in large part because they have even more appetite for change than their male counterparts. A system that excludes women, as traditional

Islam does, condemns itself to backwardness and decay. More broadly, a system that invests power into religion cannot progress if the dominant interpretation of religion is itself hostile to modernity and change.

In this context, the custom of the veil is one of the most emotional symbolic issues with which contemporary Islam has to grapple. My own country, France, has passed a law to forbid young girls to wear the veil from kindergarten through high school. I was not an enthusiastic supporter of that law, though I understood its logic. France is a country where the Jacobin tradition of extreme anticlericalism, often referred to as *laicité* (usually translated as "secularism," though it is really stronger than that), has itself become a kind of religion. But Islamic identity, including the wearing of the veil, need not be a threat to civil society. When upon my arrival in London I was met at Waterloo station by female Islamic police officers in blouses and trousers and wearing discreet veils to underline their identity, I was not shocked. I saw it instead as a triumph for tolerance and diversity.

On the other hand, the niqab or burqa, the full ensemble that completely covers the body and the face, seems to me to be in sharp contradiction with the values of the West and the requirements of daily life in our value systems. What characterizes Western civilization is the cult of the individual, and what distinguishes one person from another is precisely the face. This is why portrait painting has been so crucial to the development of Western art. Nothing is more singular and precious in this philosophy of life than the eyes of a person, "the mirror of the soul." For a Westerner, if you cannot even see the eyes of a person, she no longer exists. How can she interact in society?

The French authorities recently denied citizenship to a married woman living in France on the ground that she was wearing the niqab. I must say that I was not shocked by this decision. Tolerance for the value system of the Other should stop at the moment when we undermine our own values. Absolute cultural relativism, the idea that anyone can do what he wishes without limitation, is as great a danger as intolerance, for it leads to a sort of cynical neutrality and the loss of any value system.

Nonetheless, these are not easy problems for the West to resolve. We need to defend our own values and encourage the Arab world to soften gradually the rigidity and defensiveness that characterize its culture of humiliation. Yet how can we do this without in effect imposing our own values on them and thereby reinforcing the loss of autonomy and the sense of oppression that produced the humiliation and the resentment in the first place? I don't claim to have an easy answer to this question.

One of the dramas of the Arab world and one of the reasons for the perpetuation of the culture of humiliation is the fact that most of the leading experts on the Arab world and civilization are not Arabs themselves but Western specialists. This means that too many Arabs see their own history, if at all, through the eyes of the Other. They need to learn to approach their history in an impassioned yet possessive way, something they will be able to do only when political reforms within the Arab-Muslim world create a propitious environment for objective historical studies. As long as the reign of insecure and corrupt regimes continues, such a vital breakthrough will probably be impossible.

Political reforms, economic progress, cultural enrichment, and psychological/emotional changes are deeply interrelated. It all boils down to one issue: self-confidence.

FLASHES OF HOPE

There is a single major exception to my generalizations about the culture of humiliation in the Arab-Islamic world, a place where the necessary change in attitude is most likely to emanate from.

The Gulf emirates are a subregion that constitutes a zone of prosperity and stability in an otherwise poor and turbulent environment. Politically these emirates are classic oligarchies, where autocracy in a Bedouin tradition is tempered by the dialogue with and concern for the interests of others. The enlightened despotism of the reigning families is encouraged by their sense of fragility. Beyond the terrorist threat, always present, there is the demographic threat. With the exception of Saudi Arabia (which does not fit into the enlightened category) and Oman, the local populations represent only a small minority (15 percent in the United Arab Emirates, 20 percent in Qatar). Furthermore, one must acknowledge that the self-confidence of the emirates is somewhat artificial, based as it is on wealth fueled almost entirely by the accident of oil. It may be true that Dubai and Bahrain have expanded their economies beyond petrol to trade—some are even speaking of Dubai as the biggest money-laundering machine in the world—but it is still oil and gas that constitute the basis of their wealth and their relative freedom. Their progress is also fragile. Where will they be when the world finally outgrows its dependence on fossil fuels or when the reserves under the sands run out?

Thus, unless one is a deep believer in homeopathy, the power of a tiny influence to transform a much greater body, the emirates cannot serve as a model for the rest of the Arab-Islamic world. Their progress for the time being is spectacular but too devoid of any spiritual content to inspire anything more than envy or jealousy.

A recent sketch of life in Dubai by journalist Michael Slackman captures some of the contradictions of contemporary life in the emirates. Slackman observes:

> Dubai is, in some ways, a vision of what the rest of the
> Arab world could become—if it offered comparable
> economic opportunity, insistence on following the law
> and tolerance for cultural diversity. In this environment,
> religion is not something young men turn to because
> it fills a void or because they are bowing to a collective
> demand. That, in turn, creates an atmosphere that is open
> not only to those inclined to a less observant way of
> life, but also to those who are more religious. In Egypt,
> Jordan, Syria and Algeria, a man with a long beard is
> often treated as an Islamist—and sometimes denied work.
> Not here in Dubai.

Yet in the same article Slackman portrays the rootlessness and confusion of many of the young Muslims drawn to the emirates by economic opportunity and personal freedom. Torn between worlds, in a nominally Islamic society where pop music, fast cars, drinking, and prostitution are rampant, they come to view their "old" lives in traditional Arab cultures as stifling, yet they find their "new" lives disconnected, rudderless, and equally unsatisfying.

Someday the rapidly growing world of the emirates may develop a social structure that offers a genuine alternative to the culture of humiliation that dominates the rest of the Islamic world, but that time has not yet come.

The key country for any hope of an Arab renaissance in the foreseeable future is probably Egypt. Can the Middle Empire of the Middle East perform such a role? As the Arab power with the most significant middle class, the closest ties to the West, and the most moderate government, Egypt has the potential to provide the necessary spark. But the fact is that in the near term, this is unlikely. It is geographically located near the center of the great arc of Islamic nations stretching from the Strait of Gibraltar across the Middle East; with a population of over seventy-five million, it is the largest country in the region; and its historic role as a cradle of world civilization gives it a plausible claim to leadership. But the political conditions necessary for Egypt to give rise to an Arab Renaissance appear to be lacking. There are no strong, positive leaders ready to promote such a movement on the Egyptian stage at the moment, and no sign of such leaders waiting in the wings.

If positive reforms do not come from the heart of the Arab world, can they come from the fringes of Islam? Is a Europeanized Islam a step toward a reconciliation of the Islamist and moderate sides of Islam? Such a reconciliation would constitute a kind of normalization of Islam's internal relations, a necessary step toward normalization of Islam's relations with the rest of the world. This is not necessarily an impossible dream. It presupposes the emergence of a new generation of Muslim theologians and intellectuals willing to contribute to the creation of an enlightened Islam. It implies also the multiplication and dissemination of success stories about young European Muslims from every walk of life, from business and government to science, academia, and the arts.

Hope for these trends exists. Just consider, for example, the growing role of German directors of Turkish origins, of British directors of Indian origins, and of French directors of Algerian and Moroccan origins in the new European cinema. All of them are emerging evidence of the creativity of a Europeanized Islam.

If such a cultural renaissance does take place, European Islam could constitute a role model and a source of hope for Muslims all over the world. Extremists will always exist, but their grip on Islam today is due to the power of the culture of humiliation. Break that power by demonstrating the availability of an alternative, and a flood tide of hope may yet break over the Islamic world.

Chapter Four

THE CULTURE OF FEAR

A man who has been in danger
When he comes out of it forgets his fears,
And sometimes he forgets his promises.

—EURIPIDES, *IPHIGENIA IN TAURIS*

Our doubts are traitors
And make us lose the good we oft might win
By fearing to attempt.

—WILLIAM SHAKESPEARE, *MEASURE FOR MEASURE* (I, iv)

Fear comes third in my analysis because in my judgment, the dominant emotion of the West is above all a reaction to the events and feelings taking place elsewhere. For the first time in more than two centuries, the West is no longer setting the tune. This perception of our vulnerability and of our relative loss of centrality is at the very center of our identity crisis.

This crisis might be described in the following terms: "What's happening to us? We used to be in control of our collective lives and identities. We used to be in charge of the rest of the world. Even if, in the twentieth century, we led ourselves to self-destruction [World War I] or to suicide/murder [World War II and the Holocaust] at least we did it to ourselves. Those were our own follies. Now it seems we are to be victimized

by forces beyond our control. Asia is about to overtake us economically. Fundamentalists in the Islamic world are intent on
destroying us. Immigrants from the southern nations are about
to overwhelm us. Is there any way we can regain control of our
own destiny?"

I examine fear in a different way from how I did hope and
humiliation because in this case I am part of the culture I describe. I do not have the comfortable distance that could allow
me to focus on the essentials and to place events and feelings
into perspective. And I am not only a Westerner but also specifically a Frenchman and therefore run the risk of attributing
to other Westerners perceptions and emotions that are strictly
French. At the same time, my closeness to Western culture also
permits me to speak of it with the authority that comes from a
lifetime's experience and indeed immersion. I'll let the reader
judge whether or not I've succeeded in tempering that personal
experience with the wisdom of objectivity.

What Is Fear?

The identity crisis that confronts the Western world may be summarized by the concept of fear. But a single word may describe
very different realities. The fear that today dominates America is
quite different from that which permeates Europe. Yet it is not
an oversimplification to say that it is fear that unites the two
branches of the West, the American and European. And it is precisely the fear factor that may separate us tomorrow if America,
under the leadership of a young president, sheds its culture of
fear to recover its traditional culture of hope, while Europe, following the third no vote on Europe by the Irish people, in the
wake of the French and the Dutch noes, stumbles further into
an ever-deepening loss of confidence.

It would be a strange evolution. Could it be that at the very
moment they are coming politically closer to each other, the
United States and Europe might drift emotionally toward two
diverse emotional cultures: hope for America, fear for Europe?

The identity crisis of the Western world is still centered in the emotional reality of fear. Although Barack Obama was elected president of the United States after a campaign that explicitly promised change and hope to the American people, it is much too early to know whether he will succeed in nurturing a sense of hope that is more than a mere evanescent bubble.

Let's begin not with distinctions between the two branches of the West but with similarities. Whatever their differences, both branches face the same challenge: to acknowledge that globalization no longer belongs to them. (By contrast, the main challenge for the new powers—China, India, and Russia—is to face the fact that responsibility comes with power and they can no longer behave as international free riders.) This loss of control over the future is the shared source of fear for all the countries of the West.

If hope is confidence and humiliation is diffidence, what is fear?

In its most common interpretation, fear is an emotional response to the perception, real or exaggerated, of an impending danger. Fear leads to a defensive reflex that reveals and reflects the identity and the fragility of a person, a culture, or a civilization at a given moment. "Tell me what you are afraid of and what you are doing to transcend your fear," one might say, "and I will tell you who you are."

Fear is not only an emotional tracer but also a multifaceted reality.

Of course an element of fear is an indispensable protection against the danger of overconfidence. Fear is a force for survival in a naturally dangerous world. The rabbit that is unafraid of the hunter will not live long. The tourist who travels in the tribal zones between Afghanistan and Pakistan without taking precautions dictated by fear is an irresponsible fool. Fear stimulates attentiveness to one's surroundings and is in that sense a constructive warning, a natural protective instinct.

Fear can also be at the origins of hope. The fear of a new war between France and Germany after World War II was a decisive factor in the creation of the European Union. And fear of the consequences of global warming may yet move humankind to take the steps needed to preserve our planet from biological disaster.

But excessive fear is dangerous. An obsession with fear, either real or calculated, is a serious handicap to one's ability to interact with the world of others, either internally or externally. "Fear misleads, sometimes quite seriously. It promotes a generalized level of anxiety that is distracting at best and positively counterproductive at worst," warns historian Peter N. Stearns in his book *American Fear: The Causes and Consequences of High Anxiety.*

Has excessive fear during the last years replaced legitimate fear and begun to endanger the West's essence, its unity, and its ability to interact with the world? Has fear engendered a process of self-fulfilling prophecy?

Many people both in the United States and in Europe would bristle at such a question. Some Americans would object to the linking of the United States and Europe, preferring to differentiate Europe's "culture of weakness" from America's "culture of power." Others would argue that fear of "Islamo-Fascism" (to use a popular neoconservative term) can never be described as excessive, especially after the terrorist attacks of 9/11. Still others, more subtle, would suggest that Western leaders, particularly in the United States, might have served the public more effectively in the past decade if they had been more afraid, or at least more aware, of certain slowly growing dangers that have come to threaten global well-being, including man-made climate change and snowballing risks in the financial markets. Still others, especially in Europe, would decry any attempt to lump together all the countries of the continent under any single emotional umbrella, pointing to the real differences in the political and social responses of various European peoples to the perceived threats they face in the early years of the twenty-first century.

It would of course be more traditional and reassuring to speak of the West not in terms of fear but in terms of democracy, since democratic political institutions are supposed to be the most powerful connecting link between Europe and the United States. Unfortunately this classical vision based on values and not emotions may miss an essential novelty of our time, which is that citizens on both sides of the Atlantic today have a greatly diminished pride in their democratic models and their elected leaders (at least as reflected in confidence polls about politics and politicians in a majority of European countries as well as in the United States).

Of course citizens of democratic countries have never been shy about decrying the flaws and failings of their politicians and of the system that produces them. As Churchill famously said, "Democracy is the worst form of government, except all the others that have been tried." But today's sense of disillusionment in the democracies of the West is new, painfully real, and growing.

I think there is a connection between the fear we are suffering from and the weakening of the democratic ideal. I would go as far as to say that the culture of fear is reducing the qualitative gap that once existed between democratic and nondemocratic regimes, for fear pushes countries to violate their own moral principles based on strict respect for the rule of law. When democracies preach values they no longer practice, they lose the moral high ground and with it their power of attraction.

Of course one must also put the novelty of today's "Western fear" into an appropriate, realistic context. Fear itself is nothing new, and cycles of political and cultural fearfulness have been experienced both in Europe and in the United States. The first task of Franklin D. Roosevelt when he was elected president in 1932 was to wean the American people from the culture of fear that had seized the country as a result of the Great Depression. Similarly, the period preceding World War II in Europe was also dominated by a culture of fear, a fear of the return of war that led to blindness and passivity in the face of the rise of fascism, nazism, and Soviet communism, which of course constituted the hopes of millions of others. (Herein lay the tragedy of Europe between the wars.) A similar culture of fear swept America in the early 1950s with the explosion of McCarthyism's combination of paranoia, suspicion, and exclusion.

In the last few years a new cycle of fear, one that shares many common features in Europe and the United States, has invaded our consciousness. I do not think it actually began with 9/11, which only confirmed it and deepened it. In both regions of the West, this new cycle includes fear of the Other, the outsider who is coming to invade the homeland, threaten our identity, and steal our jobs. In both regions, it includes fear of terrorism and fear of weapons of mass destruction, the two being easily linked. It includes fear of economic uncertainty or collapse. It includes fear of natural, environmental, and organic disasters, from global warming to disease pandemics. In sum, it involves fear of an uncertain and menacing future, over which there is little, if any, possible human control. All these fears are widespread among both Europeans and Americans today.

But however similar European and American fears may appear, they stem from different realities and are expressed in different ways. They must therefore be analyzed separately before we consider how they are affecting each other and, together, impacting the world.

"Who Are We?": The European Culture of Fear

The first difficulty in defining the culture of fear of Europe is the word "Europe" itself. Are we speaking of the European Union or in broader terms of Europe as a cultural or geographic reality? Is it Europe as defined by the combined inheritance of Greece and Rome, Judeo-Christian values, and Enlightenment culture? Or is it simply the "gentlemen's club" of democracies and market economies that incarnated hope for most of the postwar period and has begun to embody fear today?

Suffice it to say that the emotion of fear dominating the European Union is having its influence beyond the confines of the union itself. "All were not dying, but all were affected," as poet Jean de La Fontaine wrote in his poem on "The animals sick with the plague." Europe's identity crisis, deepened today by the seriousness of the financial market meltdown, economic recession, and the declining purchasing power of European citizens, nonetheless predates the beginning of the subprime shock. Just watch European news on television, in particular on a French, Czech, or Italian station. Nearly every night, somewhere across the continent, there will be an attack on the rigid and anonymous decisions of a European commission that imposes financial sacrifices on various categories of workers, whether fishermen, peasants, or restaurant owners. Europe today is seen less as the solution to problems than as the source of problems, less as a source of protection than as an unwelcome imposition.

It was not always this way. In symbolic terms, the fall of the Berlin Wall in 1989 was the culmination of a European culture of hope, with people across the continent celebrating the fall of a wall that had divided them. Less than twenty years later the French and Dutch votes of no on the European constitutional treaty in 2005, followed by the Irish no in 2008, were visible signs of the emergence of a culture of fear on the European continent. Suddenly Europeans gave the impression of wishing to see the erection of walls that would separate them from the external world—its millions of competitors, its thousands of immigrants, its hundreds of terrorists. How did this change come to pass?

To understand what has happened, let's begin by glancing back at the period of European hope that began in the ashes of the end of World War II. It was a period not only of economic recovery, rebuilding, and expansion but also of spreading liberalism and freedom and steadily increasing international unity. Europe, the cradle of two global wars, became the most peaceful and prosperous region on the planet, with a powerful array of international organizations and institutions, from the Council of Europe, with its Convention on Human Rights, to the many European structures that eventually led to the European Union, including the euro. These institutions helped ensure that the benefits would be spread among an increasing number of peoples on the continent and around the world.

Yet a close examination of this period of hope shows how deeply interconnected hope and fear often are. In fact, as I alluded to before, a certain degree of fear—a fear of a return of the past and a further outbreak of armed conflict between France and Germany—actually helped drive the European Union project itself, starting with the creation of the Coal and Steel Community Pact in 1950. It was fear of Soviet tanks and fear that the outbreak of the Korean War might presage a similar conflict between communism and capitalism on European soil that encouraged the creation of the European Defense Community Plan (though it was finally rejected after Stalin's death in 1953). And it was fear of the resurgence of German nationalism and the overwhelming power that an economically vibrant Germany might wield that led to the creation of the euro.

Chancellor Helmut Kohl was crystal clear about this. He saw himself as the last "good German"—that is, the last German chancellor with personal memories of World War II. He told his partners that Europe had to hurry to complete the process of post–Cold War integration and the creation of the euro because after him, it would be too late: Fear would subside, and nationalistic self-interest would return.

This positive fear—positive in the sense that it mobilized international energies in a constructive way—was quite different from the fear that dominates Europe today. Today's fear instead produces a paralyzing effect.

Of course Europe remains a collection of countries with distinct political and social cultures, and each European country represents a unique case. Thus French fear is not to be confused with British fear, or Polish fear with German fear. Yet it remains true that fear today is Europe's "dominant color."

To understand the present archaeological layers of European fear, it is necessary first to examine the historical, political, economic, social, and psychological factors that have shaped Europe's relations with itself and its past. Only then can one analyze Europe's visions of its future in economic terms and strategic terms before returning to Europe's difficult identity quest in the present.

THE GHOSTS OF THE PAST

We must begin by reexamining the apparent high-water mark of hope, 1989. In retrospect, we can now see that the fall of the Berlin Wall, the subsequent ending of the Cold War, and the crumbling of the Soviet empire did not bring to Europe an era of peace, democracy, and prosperity, but rather the return of war in our own backyard, the Balkans.

It's difficult to overstate the devastating impact of the implosion of Yugoslavia on European self-confidence. We couldn't even figure out what it meant. Was it the sudden eruption of an

unresolved part of the European past, linked to the fact that the
Tito years in Yugoslavia had functioned as a "socialist refrigera-
tor" in which the opposition of various nationalisms had slowly
festered, dormant and unseen, for decades? Or was the return
of war to Europe a prefiguration of an ominous and potentially
fatal future?

Making matters worse, we Europeans couldn't even successfully confront this disaster by ourselves. It took the decisive
intervention of the United States to impose a fragile peace in
Bosnia and Kosovo. And today the underlying problems of Eastern Europe, with its poverty and its poisonous stew of nationalistic passions, remain largely unresolved, with countries like
Bulgaria and Romania beset with corruption charges.

Some believe the answer lies in the further enlargement of the
European Union, that gentlemen's club with its magic formula
of peace, prosperity, and ethnic reconciliation. (One might say
that to avoid the Balkanization of Europe, we must Europeanize
the Balkans—and tomorrow the Caucasus.) But most Western
Europeans have been unenthusiastic about expansion, seeing it
more as a moral and historic duty, and a political and economic
risk, than as an occasion for optimism and celebration. It can
be said that enlargement came too late emotionally (that is, too
many years after the fall of the Berlin Wall and the reunification of the European continent), and too early institutionally,
for enlargement came with the "deepening" of the union—
that is, its economic, social, and political integration—far from
completed.

Bronislaw Geremek, a great European who died in July 2008,
a leader of Solidarity and a foreign minister of Poland, used to
emphasize that Europe was not only an economic zone but also
an ethical construction that needed a heart, that needed to be
a warm community with a spiritual dimension. He was deeply
right, but how many Europeans thought or still think like him?

Strong nationalist impulses cannot be transcended easily.
Even among the founding fathers of Europe, apprehension, if
not fear, prevailed over hope. I still remember the reactions of
my friends at the Élysée Palace, the seat of the French presidency,
when a few days after the fall of the Berlin Wall I pleaded with

them for a symbolic gesture from French diplomacy. Couldn't French president François Mitterrand and Chancellor Kohl join hands at the Brandenburg Gate in Berlin, as they had done on the Verdun battlefield from World War I? In Verdun they had closed the doors of the past; in Berlin they could symbolically open the doors of the future. My idea was immediately dismissed as a "romantic move." Instead, during his trip to Germany, the French president maintained his scheduled visit to the dying regime in East Germany. The fact is that the reunification of Germany was a cause for fear, at least in certain parts of Europe. The aging and feeble Mitterrand, whose historical references predated World War II, could not help recognizing the fact that a united Germany would take a central role in the balance of power of the new Europe. Was not Warsaw much closer to Berlin than to Paris? Although he was constrained by political forces from saying so publicly, it was clear that in his mind, what was good for Germany was not necessarily good for France.

With more confidence in its destiny and its capacity to transcend its past, Europe might have greeted these new circumstances in a much more open, generous, and effective manner. But the weight of history and doubts about the essence of "Europeanness"—What does it mean to be European? Where does Europe begin and end?—were reinforced by uncertainties about the future and about Europe's economic prospects.

Economic Anxieties

As the nineties progressed, economic uncertainties plagued Europe. As a result, even routine problems became, in many minds, signs of an impending apocalypse. In countries like France and Germany, unemployment became the equivalent of a social cancer, reinforcing a dual sense of fear of the future and of the Others, who were seen as unfairly stealing jobs away from native-born Europeans. And in 2008, with the breakdown of financial markets in the United States and the spreading contagion of economic uncertainty and mistrust around the globe, economic anxiety and fear of another depression comparable to the one the world experienced in the 1930s have come to the forefront of Europeans' consciousness.

Even before the economic crisis of 2008, unemployment had been a very serious problem in Europe, especially among young people trying to enter the labor market. Psychologically it has created a sense of fragility that has passed from one generation to another, as children of parents who suffer unemployment tend to look for reassurance and are averse to risk taking. In France, recent polls have shown that nearly 75 percent of young people dream of becoming civil servants in order to have guaranteed lifetime jobs.

During the French student demonstrations of 2006 against the introduction of flexible labor laws, demonstrators interviewed on French television said they did not want "to become like Chinese or Indians." In other words, they wanted protection from the market. It was quite a change from the situation nearly forty years earlier, in May 1968, when their parents took to the streets to change a world they found boring, some of them inspired by China's Cultural Revolution. The generation of 2006 did not want to change the world but to be protected from it. The financial crisis of 2008 can only deepen this yearning for a safe haven from globalization, a safe haven that, alas, is nowhere to be found.

A French minister returning from a trip to Asia in the spring of 2008 expressed his frustration privately. He felt as if he were representing an underdeveloped country, and he said, "The Asians treated me the way we treated them in the past." Again, globalization has become an occasion for fear, equated with delocalization, job cuts, and "unfair trade," not "free trade."

Of course Europe still has its pockets of excellence, economic areas of strength, such as luxury goods and nuclear energy in France, heavy machinery in Germany, and the dynamism of family enterprises as in Italy. But will they suffice to spare the peoples of the continent from economic decline?

The fear of economic stagnation leads to yet another European fear, one that is more subtle yet quite widespread. It is the fear that Europe is condemned to become a sort of museum, a bigger equivalent of Venice, an oasis of sophisticated "good life" and culture that people from more dynamic continents enjoy visiting or retiring to, but no longer a center of creativity and influence in the world. Even if Europe (along with the world) is spared a second Great Depression, a future of quiet yet steady decline seems all too plausible.

EUROPEANS AND THE OTHER

When France and the Netherlands voted no on the European Union in 2005, and Ireland followed suit in 2008, the reasons were different in each case. But each of these no votes involved an existential malaise. There was the desire to punish the political elites in all three cases, and uneasiness with enlargement and globalization, especially in France and the Netherlands. The Irish no was particularly troubling. Ireland was the country that had most benefited from the union. The fact that it would now say no to the Treaty of Lisbon, and that the vote would be especially emphatic among the nation's young voters, was a demonstration not only of ingratitude but of deep alienation from the direction taken by the union.

I was in Berlin when I learned of the results of the Irish referendum. I wasn't surprised. Instinctively I felt that Berlin on November 9, 1989, had constituted the great victory of my generation and that June 12, 2008, was the last nail in the coffin of our dreams. The Europe I had been dreaming of since I was an adult was dead, a victim of political mediocrity and citizen alienation.

There is a sense of uncertainty over what Europe is becoming. It starts with the fear of the Other—specifically, the world's poorest, coming mostly from the south. In the minds of many Europeans, the barbarians not only are at the gates but have already swarmed over the walls and are transforming our society forever.

I still remember the amazement of a prestigious British political figure I invited to speak at the College of Europe in Natolin, Poland. I had taken him for a rapid tour of nearby Warsaw. He could not believe his eyes: All the faces he encountered were white (with the exception of a very few Asians)! Had Warsaw, freed from the Soviet orbit, become more European than London? Although he did not say so openly, I could see that he felt relieved, if perhaps slightly bored. Here at least was a remaining bastion of pure European stock, something this Englishman had assumed was gone forever.

Or consider the images coming a few years ago from the Spanish enclave of Morocco. There dozens of Africans were killed by Moroccan police as they were trying to scale barbed wire to enter our "European paradise." These terrible and powerful images, at least for someone of my generation, irresistibly evoked the images of another time not so long ago when East Germans were shot as they tried to reach freedom beyond the Berlin Wall. Today thousands of Africans risk their lives every month to escape poverty in small boats that defy the dangers of the Mediterranean Sea. These anonymous heroes include many of the best and the brightest of their continent, daring to refuse a destiny that placed them in the wrong place at the wrong time. But their dream is "our" not so secret nightmare.

The fear of the Other grows out of demography and geography. "They" are too numerous and without hope where they are. "We" are too few and so (comparatively) wealthy where we live. The more we need them for the growth of our economies (given our low birthrates), the more we reject them emotionally on cultural, religious, and racial grounds. At a certain level, diversity is no longer seen as a source of creative wealth and mutual enrichment but rather as a source of internal destabilization. In Switzerland, the image of the "black sheep" used by the extreme right to single out immigrants in the last electoral campaign in 2007 caught the imagination. In France, Nicolas Sarkozy successfully wooed away Jean-Marie Le Pen's far-right supporters by promising to fight illegal immigration vigorously, a promise he is fulfilling as president with an energy that spells long-term human rights problems as well as economic difficulties for France.

As exaggerated in the minds of the most fearful Europeans, fear of the Other expands to include actual conquest by the Islamic world, the possibility that Europe will be demographically and religiously conquered by "them" and transformed into "Eurabia" (a term used by the late Italian journalist Oriana Fallaci, the American historian Walter Laqueur, and the prominent Orientalist Bernard Lewis).

This fear of "Eurabia" is not supported by facts. In their excellent essay on France and its Muslims, *Integrating Islam: Political and Religious Challenges in Contemporary France*, Jonathan Laurence and Justin Vaïsse give revealing statistics. As they demonstrate, the great majority of European Muslims—Germans of Turkish origin; French of Algerian, Moroccan, or Tunisian origin; and British of Indo-Pakistani origin—want to integrate successfully in their respective countries. They expect to be given opportunities to rise in society and to be treated fairly, even with a sense of fraternity. In fact integration is a reality, even in the most intimate form, through marriage, with some 40 percent of European Muslims marrying outside their community of origin.

In the seven years I taught at the College of Europe in Poland, some of my very best students were Franco-Algerians. They wanted to make it as French or, as one of them told me, "at least as European." But are we treating them in a fair, open, and (most difficult) fraternal way?

Fear of the Other also includes the fear of terrorism, especially as embodied in the image of the bomb-carrying Muslim fundamentalist. Fear of terrorism in Europe is not the result of a single massive trauma, as in the United States. Terrible as they were, the terrorist attacks on Madrid in 2005 and London in 2006 (as well as the failed attempts of 2007 in Great Britain) were on a lesser scale than the 9/11 attack in New York. Furthermore, Irish and Basque terrorists had already inured Europeans to terrorism and toughened their skin. And in a sense, European citizens do not exist. At heart a majority of Europeans may feel less for Madrid and London than they felt at least for a short while for New York after 9/11 (when headlines proclaimed WE ARE ALL NEW YORKERS).

Nonetheless, Europeans have gradually come to face the hard reality that Europe is not only a target for terrorists but also a base for them. For many of the English after July 2006, the greatest shock was the realization that the enemy was within them; in fact the enemy *was* them. The suicide bombers of London were mostly British citizens born and educated in Great

Britain. By the same token, most of the 9/11 hijackers had gone through technical universities in Europe. Living with Europeans and being taught by European professors had not distracted them from their terrible project. It is clear that our universities had absolutely no humanistic appeal for them, either in the contents of the courses they took or in any marginal attempts to integrate them culturally and socially.

These facts underscore the vulnerability and weakness of Europe in the face of hatred from the Islamic world. But they must be placed in perspective. To neglect the existence of a threat would be suicidal, but to be obsessed with it is counterproductive, for our ambition must be to integrate migrants of every faith and background as successfully as possible. After all, we need them as much as they need us.

Finally, there is the fear of being ruled by an outside power. This power might be a friendly one, like the United States; it might be a not so friendly power, like Russia; it might be an anonymous, nonelected bureaucracy like the European Commission in Brussels. The first possibility obviously used to cause greater anxiety in France (at least before the coming to power of Nicolas Sarkozy in France and of Barack Obama in the United States), the second in Poland, the third in Britain. The European Commission lately has tended to be seen more and more in the public eye as a kind of twenty-eighth nation of Europe, one with its specific and distinct national interests, rather than as the incarnation of the common good of Europe. But what unites all these fears is the fear of loss of control over one's own destiny.

WHO ARE WE?

Europe's sense of uncertainty is made worse by the lack of clear geographic borders. Combined with the failure of the European Union to develop a clear sense of identity, purpose, and direction for the collection of nations it embraces, this has undoubtedly had a negative impact on Europe's psychological borders. Who are we? Europeans have no clear answer to the question of where their continent begins and ends. What about Ukraine?

The countries of the Caucasus, such as Georgia? Countries on the other side of the Mediterranean, such as Morocco? Can France and Algeria become pillars of a reconciliation process between the two shores of the Mediterranean, as advocated with such passion by France's President Sarkozy? And what about a country that is undoubtedly Western if not European: Israel?

This anxiety over the borders of Europe finds its current emotional center in the dispute over Turkey. With the possible exception of Britons, the majority of European citizens are clearly hostile to the entrance of Turkey as a full member in the union. Turkey is not perceived as the "European Other" but as the "non-European Other." In France, this hostility is simply overwhelming, with polls showing 75 percent of the French opposed to the entrance of Turkey into the European Union.

This opposition cannot be understood in purely rational terms. It does not stem only from political, economic, or even demographic concerns. It is above all the product of fear of the very numerous and absolute Other—the Muslim—that Turkey incarnates. It is the fear of seeing eighty million Muslims, wrongly perceived by the average Frenchman as Arabs, invading our "Christian" yet secular place.

The rational arguments in favor of Turkey's entrance into the union were, if anything, strengthened by the events of 9/11. The need for a strategic and diplomatic partner that significantly reinforces the clout of Europe in the Middle East, the message of reconciliation sent to Islam, the dynamism of a youthful Turkey: All these argue in favor of Turkish membership. So does the current political evolution of Turkey, in which the Kemalist ideology founded by Atatürk (centered on modern, secular reforms driven by a benign military authoritarianism) is giving way to new energies driven by Islamic social mores and increased demands for popular democracy. Under current circumstances, to close the doors of Europe to Turkey forever would be to take a great historical risk, pushing back the inheritors of the Ottoman Empire into their Asian, Muslim, and Middle Eastern destiny.

It is true that Turkey's democratic credentials are not overly impressive. But in purely economic terms, Istanbul has more right to be in the European Union than Sofia or Bucharest. And in the question of Turkish accession to the union, the journey is more important than the destination. The reforms Turkey has been able to implement in a very short period of time thanks to its candidacy to the union can only be described as impressive. Can we take the historic risk of blocking that positive process by the expression of a definitive no?

Emotionally of course I understand the concerns of opponents of the Turkish entry into the union. It would turn Syria and Iraq into bordering states of the union. And culturally Turkey is undoubtedly a non-European country. Even in Istanbul, the most Westernized of Turkish cities, as soon as one leaves the main arteries, one seems to be immersed in a Middle Eastern or Asian place. To want "Turkey in" is an act of will and political intelligence that is in many ways, I admit, counterintuitive.

Yet in the end I unhesitatingly favor inclusion. Without the prospect of union membership, the temptation of the East could prove irresistible for Turkey. As a result, the union would find itself with a potentially very problematic neighbor.

Even more important are the questions of identity that the Turkish dilemma poses. Is the union based on culture or politics? The question is less clear than ever and offers a perfect illustration of the growing confusion that exists between Europe at large and the European Union. In the long term, multiple identities are acceptable only if you feel at ease with your core identity. If not, the tendency to reject the imposition of an artificial foreign culture on your core culture will become irresistible. For multiculturalism to be a working formula, it must be practiced with self-confidence.

For this and other reasons, a sense of alienation toward the union has grown within the various member countries of Europe. France no longer feels like the head of the family when it sits at the table of the Ministerial Councils. In this new Europe there are so many new faces one does not recognize, so many new languages one cannot even distinguish, so few minutes to express one's position, between Malta and Slovenia! It is difficult for Paris to maintain the illusion that Europe is the "pursuit of national goals through other means" when so many compromises have to be accepted.

Meanwhile, though Germany at times looks and behaves like "a second France," it is unwilling to sacrifice what it perceives as its national interest for the sake of some abstract European cause. Though guided by a new generation of leaders less burdened by the history of Nazi guilt, Germany remains the most European nation of all, as if twelve years of barbarism had constituted some kind of vaccination against the evils of nationalism. But Germany cannot move Europe alone.

Would Europe's sense of self-confidence be greater if the threatened nationalism of individual countries had been replaced by a unifying patriotism directed toward the entire continent? We'll never know, since the founders of the European Union deliberately chose not to foster such a continental patriotism. Jacques Delors, who headed the union from the mid-eighties to the mid-nineties and was perhaps its most remarkable president, was passionately opposed to the creation of such a "European emotion." For him, "Patriotism meant war." As a result of this negative vision, one fears that national emotions are returning with a vengeance, with the existence of a commonality of national interests as the only rational barrier to limit their negative impact.

I attended the ceremony in Warsaw celebrating the entrance of Bulgaria and Romania into the European Union. National anthems were performed with fervor and emotion, while the anthem of the union, the "Ode to Joy" from Beethoven's Ninth Symphony, was played with a discreet indifference. The difference symbolizes the emotional gulf between our national identities and our identities as Europeans.

To recover confidence in itself, Europe has to work harder and to grow faster. The current differential in economic growth between Europe and Asia spells disaster in the long run. As long as the West is the hemisphere of debt and the East is the hemisphere of growth (even growth at a reduced rate), continuing European decay will be inexorable.

THE AMERICAN CULTURE OF FEAR

If it is difficult to define Europe, it is equally difficult to define America. Blue America versus red America, rich America versus poor America, rural America versus urban America, Main Street America versus Wall Street America, white America versus black America (the last a distinction that seemed especially real in the aftermath of Hurricane Katrina in 2005): One could multiply the kaleidoscope of radically different realities that constitute America.

Here is another way of dividing America: One could say that there is one America united by fear and another united by the fear of fear and that the latter America has rallied under the banner of hope. From that standpoint, the 2008 presidential campaign can be seen as a confrontation between the candidate of fear, John McCain, and the candidate of hope, Barack Obama.

The negative campaign of the Republican Party was aimed at evoking and exacerbating social, cultural, and economic fears. Can you trust a man with so little experience and whose middle name, Hussein, is so characteristically Muslim? Do "elite" opinion makers in cities like Washington, New York, Boston, and Los Angeles care about the values and needs of blue-collar workers and small-business owners in the American heartland? Is anyone prepared to defend traditional American cultural values against the transforming tide of global capitalism? Fears like these have been familiar political weapons in the United States for the past generation, but the 2008 election saw them awarded a central role in the Republican campaign.

By contrast, the Kennedy-like style of Obama evoked the culture of hope in America. Democratic optimism about the 2008 election was based on the assumption that by the end of the day, despite Obama's handicaps of age and skin color, Americans, because they are Americans, would choose the youthful "color of hope." Obama's victory may come to be seen as a significant turning point in American history—a decisive shift away from fear and toward a new version of American hope—although it will take more than an electoral victory, however impressive, to ratify such a shift.

In describing the American culture of fear, I am keenly aware of a specific difficulty. Who am I to speak?

While I am not an American, I have a very personal relationship with this country. I was a student at Harvard in the early 1970s, which some of my readers may see as more of a liability than an advantage. But America means much more to me than just a source of an education. America gave me life, hope, and dreams. Americans freed my father from a German concentration camp on May 8, 1945, and thereby made my own birth possible. America also allowed my dreams to come true, for my student years at Harvard changed my life in more than one way.

Sadly, the America that I saw between 2001 and 2008 did not bear much resemblance to the America that helped mold my life. Thus in the case of America I am not a neutral observer but more of a disappointed lover. I am prepared to take chances in my account of this country because of this emotional connection, which means so much to me.

When I look at the United States today, I see a country that, like Europe, is insecure and fearful, though the roots of that fear are rather different.

Unlike Europeans, Americans are not preoccupied by the ghost of their past. America has always seen itself as a future, a project more than a history. Three key questions contribute to the current American identity crisis. Have we lost our soul—that is, our ethical superiority? Have we lost our purpose—that is, our sense of a unique national mission? Finally, have we lost our place in the world—that is, are we in decline? (This last question is of course a classic one, which Yale historian Paul Kennedy was asking as long ago as 1987. Perhaps he was simply twenty years ahead of his time.)

In other words, if Europeans are asking, "Who are we?" Americans are wondering, What have we done to ourselves? They are seeking an answer to the questions, Why do they hate us so? and Why do our former friends and allies dislike and distrust us? Has the whole world turned against us without cause? Or have we ceased to be the country that the world once loved and admired?

In this process of self-questioning, Americans are starting to challenge the universalism and centrality of their own model and system. What is good for America may not be good for the rest of the world. What's more, since Americans have largely stopped practicing the values they preach, how can they even know what is good for them?

WHAT HAVE WE DONE TO OURSELVES?

To analyze the culture of fear in America, one must not start with 9/11. Fear has always been present in American history, with the witchcraft terror of the seventeenth century one of its clearest early illustrations. America's conquest of its territory was accompanied by violence—against the native Indians and the enslaved Africans, of course, but above all among fellow pioneers. The free circulation of guns that remains characteristic of the United States to this day not only celebrates individualism and self-defense but also represents the inheritance of a wild, violent, and dangerous past, where "man is wolf to man" and fear was a natural part of life.

In the first half of the twentieth century, the upsurge in communism, radicalism, anarchism, bombings, strikes, violence, and labor unrest led to widespread fear of all immigrants, who were seen by many Americans as threats to the nation's social and political stability. This antialien hysteria reached a peak in the Red Scare of 1919–1920 and a generation later in the dark excesses of the McCarthy period of the 1950s.

Fear did not vanish with the successful conclusion of World War II. The Reagan victory in 1980 was at least in part the product of a counterrevolutionary backlash against the moral and cultural "excesses" of the 1960s, seen by many as a time of unabashed sexual freedom, drug use, and political unrest. For Reagan's voters, America in 1980 had lost control of the world and its destiny, just as American parents had lost control of their adolescent children. Something had to be done about it.

This diagnosis solidified a forty-year-long battle within the baby boom generation, between the "Woodstock generation" who opposed the war in Vietnam and those who fought and supported it. It's a conflict that is still at the heart of American cultural and political debates. This division and the fear of national decadence and decline it inspires among many conservatives help explain the prominence of cultural and moral issues (abortion, gay rights, school prayer) over economic and political ones in several recent presidential campaigns (although not in 2008).

So the terror attacks of 9/11 did not create American fear, but they encapsulated and heightened it through the power of a singular event: the large number of casualties and the symbolic nature of the targets (the heart of U.S. military power and the Twin Towers, which dominated the skyline of the most cosmopolitan of all cities, the center of capitalism and multiculturalism). On top of it, there was the timing. America rediscovered its own vulnerability at the peak of its global supremacy, just a decade after the collapse of the Soviet Union. Never since the British attack on Washington in the War of 1812 had America experienced such an attack at its very heart (Pearl Harbor was far away from the homeland).

Though 9/11 did not create the American culture of fear, it gave it a new depth. Americans had known since the beginning of the Cold War that their geographic position no longer protected them. But 9/11 changed an abstract knowledge into a tragic, visceral reality. And in the American way it launched an immediate debate on the nature of the American response.

Many of those, like me, who felt themselves to be New Yorkers on 9/11 have been questioning America's judgment in the wake of the attacks. We wonder whether the United States underestimated the threat before 9/11 and overestimated it after, whether it has been waging in Iraq the wrong war in the wrong manner, and whether it has been creating a climate of suspicion detrimental to the image and the interests of the United States.

The debate between security and liberty is an eternal one. In its "global war on terror," the Bush administration has failed to find the right balance. Guantánamo, "preventive detention," and the harsh interrogation techniques and deliberate humiliation of prisoners at Abu Ghraib have helped create a sense of abuse and victimization among those who run afoul of American justice. They symbolize, sadly, what has gone wrong with America in the wake of 9/11.

In 2008, I experienced firsthand the dramatic shifts in the image of the United States in the city of Berlin. In June, I saw at the

Unter den Linden Berlin Opera a performance of Beethoven's homage to freedom and love, Fidelio. The staging of the opera, however, contained a stark political commentary. The prisoners (supposed to be captives in a Spanish political prison) were dressed like detainees at Guantánamo. In the artistic imagination of the director, America had come to incarnate oppression.

More than twenty years earlier I had accompanied to the opera (on the western side of the still-divided city) John McCloy, the American "proconsul" in Berlin in the years following World War II. Learning of McCloy's presence in the hall, the audience had stood up spontaneously to give him a warm, prolonged ovation. America then was a symbol of freedom, liberation, and even redemption for West Germans. How had America's image changed so brutally from freedom to oppression?

(Of course the same city triumphantly welcomed presidential candidate Barack Obama in July 2008, just one month after the grim production of Fidelio that I attended. Had another shift begun?)

In his very convincing book Winning the Right War: The Path to Security for America and the World, Philip H. Gordon denounces the temptation to equate the war on terror with World War III, the illusion that it can be won like a traditional war, and the idea that there is no middle ground between "victory or holocaust," which is the way two experts close to the Bush administration, David Frum and Richard Perle, argue in their book An End to Evil: How to Win the War on Terror.

Seeing "evil" everywhere means closing the country on itself, as every foreigner who has experienced the frustrations of America's new security apparatus while entering the country can attest. (Not that Europe is immune to such excesses. In the immediate aftermath of 9/11 and the major terrorist attacks in Madrid and London, it was certainly better not to be a young bearded Muslim when traveling in Europe.)

Encouraged by the "Bolsheviks of democracy" (the provocative formula created by the former French student leader Daniel Cohn-Bendit to describe the American neoconservatives), the Bush administration found in 9/11 a unique opportunity to rally Americans to their muscular brand of internationalism. But in its new approach the United States combined overambition with overreaction. The goal of democratizing the Middle East was perfectly noble in itself, but the idea of building it with a new democratic Baghdad as its epicenter was sheer illusion. To glimpse the ethical soul-searching millions of Americans are now engaging in, we can turn to Hollywood, whose movies have always represented a kind of national psychoanalytic program. In the powerful final scene of In the Valley of Elah, a father whose son has been butchered upon his return to America from Iraq by his own comrades in arms, maddened by the war, raises the American flag upside down, a symbol of emergency and distress. The implied message: "My country has gone insane. Please help us!"

THE FADING AMERICAN DREAM

In contrast with Europe, America has traditionally been characterized above all by hope. Its very history (like that of the state of Israel) is based on an almost messianic hope, a belief in America as a land of redemption, liberation, and new beginnings. It is this hopeful optimism that has enabled the modest, plain-living, idealistic early American Republic to grow to imperial status in less than two centuries. That same spirit of hope has remained the basis of America's soft power and its enormous attractiveness to people around the world as well.

Of course the power to attract immigrants and to seduce the world is based as much on the attractiveness of the American dream as on the achievements of the American Republic. Optimism, idealism, individualism, flexibility, the cult of excellence, and the conviction of being unique have traditionally constituted the key ingredients of success for a country that saw itself from the start as a project in construction rather than a memory or a tradition to protect or to transcend. Where twentieth-century Europe was built on the idea of transcending history, its special strength and weakness being its ability to evoke or to conjure up its past, America is above all about the future.

The Hollywood dream that is America was perfectly encapsulated in the movie *Pelle the Conqueror* by the Danish director Billie August. Set in Nordic Europe at the end of the nineteenth century, the film concludes with the parting of two brothers who have chosen different ways to escape the absolute poverty in which they live. The first chooses socialism and seeks to transform Europe from within. The second leaves the European continent to pursue the American dream. The implicit message of the film is that the second brother has made the right choice. This contrast, with the flattering light it casts on America's self-image, is the underlying theme of most great American movies: "If you can dream it, you can do it." From *Shane* and *Casablanca* to *Working Girl* and *Norma Rae*, it is the power of the individual that is magnified in American cinema and in the American way of life.

I remember being in Washington on the eve of the U.S. military intervention in Kosovo. A key policy maker at the State Department explained to me that "his folks in California did not like to see people forced into trains in Europe." It would be excessive to conclude from that exchange that the popularity of Steven Spielberg's epic film *Schindler's List* was responsible for the American military intervention, but it certainly played a role in preparing the public to support the action.

But now some Americans are starting to doubt the unique value of America's individualism. In a recent column written from China, David Brooks asks a very pertinent question: What will happen if "collectivist societies rise economically and come to rival the West"? He concludes by saying that the "rise of China is not only an economic event. It's a cultural one. The ideal of a harmonious collective may turn out to be as attractive as the ideal of the American dream."

No one contributed more to this rise of self-doubt than Americans themselves. Let us compare for an instant the present with the past. In symbolic terms at least, D-day (June 6, 1944) remains the high mark of American idealism, enlightenment, and heroism. The monument at the entrance of the gigantic cemetery of Colleville in Normandy above Omaha Beach says it all: "This embattled shore, portal of freedom, is forever hallowed by the ideals, the valor and the sacrifices of our fellow countrymen." For the second time in less than thirty years, American soldiers altered the course of European and world history for the better.

What followed in subsequent American wars was much less brilliant and decisive. The Korean War was a murky stalemate; the Vietnam War was a tragedy and a political disaster for the United States. Will America's finest moment prove to be a high point it will never again experience?

By comparison with the images and historical memories of World War II, the present war in Iraq appears even more bleak than Korea or Vietnam. And the aftermath of the war is likely to bear no resemblance to that of World War II, for Iraq will never become the equivalent of Germany and Japan in 1945. These two nations were eager to learn from the democratic models of the United States, to transcend their recent history, to immerse themselves in another culture, to be reborn afresh. Iraq shares none of these positive traits.

But even more fundamentally, America in 2003 had little in common with America in 1944. The mostly very young soldiers who landed on Omaha and Utah beaches knew what they were doing and were ready to sacrifice their lives for a cause they understood and believed in. They were supported by political and military establishments they trusted. They were convinced that their commanders would lead them to victory, and they were sure their country was doing its utmost to help them fight a war in the best possible conditions. Is this still the case today? Do American soldiers have the right guidance, the right equipment, the right morale? Stories coming out of Iraq sound more like the Vietnam-era tales of cynicism, confusion, and failure than the heroic sagas of World War II. Furthermore, the U.S. military today is a professional force composed mainly of poor Americans who enrolled to get a job, fighting next to highly paid private contractors who are in Iraq for the money. War is never pretty, but the soldiers of World War II rested on a bedrock of idealism that is hard to discern in today's American army.

Has America, the land of hopes and dreams, lost its sense of unique mission and become, like Europe, a land of fear?

AN AMERICA IN DECLINE

Is America at the start of the twenty-first century the equivalent of the British Empire a century ago or the Roman Empire in its centuries of decadence?

Americans have been debating the issue of decay for a long time. The success of Fareed Zakaria's last essay, *The Post-American World*, shows how timely the subject is. I basically share Zakaria's reassuring thesis that America can survive "the rise of the rest," the rest being essentially Asia. America's dynamism, resilience, and adherence to a cult of excellence remain strong, and its ability to rebound from economic and social troubles is probably greater than that of Europe.

Yet the reality of American decay is seeping in, taking several forms: the organic, physical form of the plague of obesity; the budgetary form of spiraling debt too long overlooked; the crumbling of American infrastructure, from bridges to railways, which sometimes evokes a developing nation of the global south more than the world's leading power; the lack of appetite of U.S. soldiers for foreign adventures; the rising drug use, violence, and aimlessness among the young; the out-of-control financial markets, which finally collapsed in the fall of 2008, threatening to bring down the world's economy with them; and above all the dysfunctional nature of American politics, from the unchecked growth of executive power to the excessive amount of money poured into elections.

In the latter years of the 2000s, with debt markets shutting down, the stock market in retreat, and economic growth rates falling to European levels, Americans are starting to fear economic decay as Europeans do. Like Europeans, they worry about job cuts and being "owned" by companies from China or other foreign powers. One senses something like a backlash against globalization and the return of strong protectionist tendencies, further reinforced by environmental anxieties.

As seen from Europe, America looks like a land of excessive controls at the frontiers and insufficient ones inside. And the insufficient controls don't include only failed regimes for regulating financial markets. They include lax systems for moderating social behaviors and mitigating the worst effects of rampant individualism. Consider, for example, the emphasis on the right to bear arms, which leads to the availability of firearms as a permanent Damocles' sword hanging over the heads of so many innocent Americans, given the multiplication of shooting sprees at American high schools, colleges, and universities. Is there another country in the world where teachers are authorized, if not encouraged, to come to high school classes armed with a gun, as they are in Texas? And Europeans worry that this lack of control is spreading to Europe, a disheartening form of Americanization that includes youthful violence modeled on the gang wars taking place in too many American cities and the rise of excessive alcohol consumption.

Have the feelings and realities of an earlier, more hopeful America simply ceased to exist in the United States, or is the moment we live in a temporary aberration?

Reasons for optimism do exist, rooted not merely in the potential for change embodied in Barack Obama but in certain fundamental values that have long characterized the people of the United States. Perhaps America, the quintessential nation of immigrants, will find new energies and transcend its fears thanks to the millions of new citizens arriving on its shores every year. America is rightly proud to be the land of the melting pot and the successful integration of peoples from around the world. During World War II, in spite of confinement and segregation, Americans of Japanese descent served with honor in special contingents of the U.S. Army. Today the same tradition continues. Just compare the largely successful integration of American Hispanics with the difficulties being experienced by the Muslim and black communities in Europe. And in spite of 9/11, the American Muslim community has continued to strive economically and to feel and act as Americans much more successfully than its European counterparts have managed to be integrated into European life.

Most responsible U.S. leaders recognize the value of this tradition. Key politicians from both sides of the aisle, such as President George W. Bush and Senator Edward Kennedy, remain convinced that immigration is a boon to the United States, that "newcomers bring a welcome vitality, and that openness and optimism are a critical part of the nation's character," as Tamar Jacoby has written in *Foreign Affairs*. When thoughtful Americans say that the only plausible remedy to illegal immigration is more generous quotas combined with more effective law enforcement, they sound somewhat more credible than some of their European counterparts such as Nicolas Sarkozy in France, who has so far failed to find the balance between generosity and control.

Yet of course not all is well in the nation of immigrants. Visas for students have been severely reduced in the last eight years, and the controls imposed on "foreigners" have been drastically increased. America will harm its future if it ceases to be the place of choice for immigrants.

It is easy to overstate the potential for a new presidential administration to reshape the nation's emotional landscape. However intelligent, competent, and inspirational he may be, there is a limit to what a chief executive can accomplish in four or eight years in the White House. But if President Obama is truly committed to restoring America's image as the land of all possibilities, he has this on his side: that he is striving not against but with the national grain, seeking not to innovate but rather to restore his country's traditional view of itself, in which a strong belief in ethical values, an instinctive faith in moderation, and a bracing dose of realism combine to produce a quiet, healthy sense of optimism. Such a restoration, if it happens, will be welcomed throughout the world.

FEAR DIVIDES THE WEST

Fear has not only harmed both Europe and the United States but also harmed their relationship. The disaster of 9/11 united people on both sides of the Atlantic. But except for a few key collaborations (for example, between police and justice systems), this sense of shared purpose lingered only briefly. September 11 did not permanently reunite the West but rather revealed its deep divisions. And President Bush's foreign policy choices and style widened the chasm that had begun to open with the collapse of the Soviet empire.

As the Cold War came to an end, Aleksandr Yakovlev, a close collaborator of President Gorbachev's, in a prescient remark, warned the West, "We are going to do something terrible to you; we are going to disappear as a threat. The glue of your alliance will no longer be there to keep you united." The apparent dilution of common interests brought about by the end of the Cold War is coinciding with the growth of diverging emotions, for unless the nature of fear is absolutely clear, it divides more than it unites. During the Cold War the external threat was well defined and, thanks to nuclear deterrence, well contained. (This was at least the perception; the reality was probably more confused and more dangerous than it appeared at the time.) Today's reality is more confused. What is the primary threat? Is it potential economic collapse, weapons of mass destruction, the spread of political chaos in failed states, global warming, or the energy crisis? Complexity rarely gives birth to strategic clarity and certainly not to emotional certainty.

The transatlantic divorce has not been an event but a process. It slowly grew in the 1990s and exploded in the first years of the twenty-first century. It predated the accession of President George W. Bush, the war in Iraq, and the deep divisions it created. To summarize this rift, one can say that America's scorn for Europe grew while Europe felt it needed America less. At the same time, America seemed to be moving away from Europe in terms of fundamental values. It was as if Europe were saying to America, "I can live without your protection now. And what's worse, I don't recognize you anymore." (Of course this was the perception of "Old Europe" much more than of the "New Europe" of nations from the former Soviet bloc, which resemble the Europe of the 1970s much more than that of the 1990s.)

American disillusion with Europe was growing at the same time. The war in the Balkans and the initial poor performance of the Europeans there confirmed the deepest suspicions of many in the American elite. I remember a debate I had in Strasbourg with a key member of the National Security Council at the very beginning of the 1990s, when Yugoslavia was still united. That high representative of the George H. W. Bush presidency spoke of Europe in the most derogatory terms: "You cannot trust Europe. Leave her alone. She will first prove to be divided and impotent, then she will turn suicidal, and America will have to intervene once more to save her from herself and to pick up the pieces."

America's disbelief in Europe's capacity to get its act together, reinforced by the first years of the war in the Balkans, was rapidly matched by Europe's growing alienation from the United States. In the 1960s and 1980s, when Europeans marched in the streets against the United States, they were denouncing the actions of Washington, from the Vietnam War to the deployment of Euromissiles. In the 1990s, anti-American demonstrations were aimed not so much at what America *did* as at what America *was*: a cultural swamp, a country where the death penalty ruled, a powerful but inhumane and, some might even say, uncivilized corner of the West.

This reading of America did not suppress the concomitant existence of an absolute fascination with the United States that was still growing in a country like France. I still remember a double-page spread that ran in the leading French Sunday newspaper *Le Journal du Dimanche*. On the right-hand page appeared the description of a young French couple living in Los Angeles, having joined the "Land of dream and opportunity," in the realm of the "new economy." On the left-hand page you could read a strong denunciation of American capitalism by a leading antiglobalization voice. This double vision said it all. America was the perfect mirror reflecting both the dreams and the nightmares of France and, by extension, those of all Europe.

After 9/11, fear largely replaced hope in the European vision of the United States. Europeans and Americans were united against the threat of terrorism, but their divisions over the best way to fight the enemy became larger than the threat itself. For Washington, Europeans were "traitors" when they did not support the choices of U.S. leaders. For Europeans, America became as great a threat to the stability of the world as the terrorists themselves, for the "overreaction" of Washington was paving the way to a needless and potentially fatal "clash of civilizations." Stereotypes on both sides of the Atlantic—American cowboys and gangsters, European cowards and decadents—were fed by a combination of ignorance and growing intolerance. But whereas Europe's prejudices toward America were fed by passion, America's denunciation of Europe's weaknesses was accompanied by a growing indifference.

In truth the attitudes of both sides were deeply contradictory. Washington spoke of the importance of Western values, such as democracy and human rights, even as it violated those principles and betrayed its contempt for its "junior partner," the Europe that had originated those same values. Meanwhile Europe looked to America for stability and protection while being obviously pleased with the weakening of the United States and the deterioration of its image in the world, a senseless attitude, since Europe is probably still not ready to accept a greater role in the world and the costly burden sharing that would entail.

Despite these internal contradictions, the rift between the erstwhile partners continued to grow. The defiant criticism of America long voiced by France was now echoed in a majority of European and world capitals. (Today, under the presidency of Nicolas Sarkozy, there is a new relationship between Paris and Washington. But the French are less enthusiastic than their president and have been waiting anxiously for the election of a new president in the United States to change their mind about America.) Only in the non-Muslim countries of Asia has the popularity of the United States remained high. If Americans woke up the morning after 9/11 wondering for the first time, Why do our enemies hate us so much? today they need to ask, "Why have we become so unpopular even among our friends?"

Some might answer this question by pointing to the notion that in its bid for world supremacy, the United States has "betrayed the American promise" (to quote the subtitle of Tony Smith's last book, *A Pact with the Devil: Washington's Bid for World Supremacy and the Betrayal of the American Promise*). There is some truth in this. The greatest success of al Qaeda has been to move America under the Bush administration to betray its own fundamental values.

But I would express what has happened somewhat differently. In moving from a culture of hope to a culture of fear, America has lost its natural appeal to the world. John Fitzgerald Kennedy, for all his limitations, made the world dream. George W. Bush's America has tended to scare the world, even if some of the fear it has generated is excessive and unfair.

"Americans' faith in our values, universal values, should be a bridge to the world," says Anne-Marie Slaughter in her elegant book *The Idea That Is America: Keeping Faith with Our Values in a Dangerous World*. This can still be true, despite the anxiety that currently dominates Western thinking. Neither America's estrangement from the world nor Europe's weakness need prove fatal. What the West needs is a greater sense of balance, including both a more restrained America and a more ambitious Europe, an America less ambitious about mastering the world and more ambitious about restoring itself, with a reinforced emphasis on education, infrastructure, and social welfare.

In a transparent, interdependent world, it is the resurgence of the American dream—the continuing capacity to integrate others and personify the land of hope—that constitutes America's most attractive face toward the rest of the world and toward Europe in particular.

The greater responsibility rests upon the shoulders of the stronger of the two partners, America. If the West is to recover its culture of hope, it will be because the United States has finally found the leader who can serve as the bridge between America and its past of hopes and dreams and the world of the twenty-first century.

For the West to lose its monopoly on hope is one thing, probably inevitable. To be reduced to being the new center of fear need not prove fatal, but without a positive change of course, it could be.

Chapter Five

Hard Cases

Although there are many varying hues and shades of color in the portrait of the contemporary world that I am analyzing, I hope I am succeeding in demonstrating that in general terms, the Asian world today is characterized especially by hope, the Arab-Islamic world by humiliation, and the Western world by fear.

But there are some very important countries that elude my simple three-part classification precisely because they contain all three emotions equally or in deeply intermingled proportions. And there are regions of the world, including entire continents, that are even more difficult to assign to any simple categories. In this chapter I concentrate on a number of complex situations that don't neatly fit my broader thesis but that have their own significant role to play in the gradually unfolding struggles of the coming century.

The Russian Amalgam (with a Word About Iran)

The case of Russia in these post-Soviet times is definitely one of the most interesting and atypical. The country possesses at the same time more than its share of fear, humiliation, and hope, all three emotions mixing in a powerful amalgam of feelings and impulses.

I vividly remember being in Moscow in the winter of 1989, staying with Russian friends and watching the news from Romania as it was unfolding. The revolution—or was it a coup?—ended tragically, in dark contrast with the relatively peaceful transition from communism to capitalism experienced by Poland and, in time, by the rest of Central and Eastern Europe. As the television screen flashed images of the execution of Nicolae Ceauşescu and his wife, who had brutally ruled the country for more than twenty years, my Russian friends turned to me. "You know," they warned me, "the transition in Russia is going to be the Romanian, not the Polish, way. Blood will be spilled. This is how we do things in Russia."

They proved to be wrong, at least for the time being. Their attitude, which I like to call dark narcissism, nevertheless stuck with me because I have encountered it so many times since.

Why are Russians, in spite of their undeniable if fragile progress at least in economic terms, so obsessed with their tragic failings and flaws? What combination of geography, history, religion, and culture makes them so proud and so ashamed at the same time?

The first explanation comes from the fact that Russians have no clear vision about their borders. Where does their empire end? Deep down they have not given up on Ukraine or, for that matter, on Belorussia. The complex and inflated web of emotions that characterizes the Russians can be seen as the result of their national history and their paradoxical sense of attraction and rejection toward a West they are not a natural part of. The debate between "Westernizers" and "Slavophiles" (the latter group convinced that Russia's "soul" and destiny are to be found in the mystic East rather than the rationalist West) has dogged modern Russian history ever since the time of Peter the Great, and it persists to this day.

When Putin came to Paris in 2000 for his first official visit as the newly elected president of Russia, I had the opportunity to speak with him at a dinner in his honor hosted by the French Institute for International Relations. Puzzling over what to ask

Putin that might both interest him and enlighten the audience, I decided to ask what portraits of leaders, past and present, he had in his office. His answer came so quickly that I realized this was a question he had reflected upon before. "There are three," he told me. "Peter the Great, Pushkin, and de Gaulle." The first of course was the father of the modern Russian empire and state, the second was the incarnation of Russian culture, and the third was the man responsible for the reconstruction of France after World War II and the country's renewed sense of importance on the world stage. The choice of de Gaulle was, I thought, a revealing one that said a lot about Putin's view of his own challenge as the leader of contemporary Russia. De Gaulle too had felt humiliated by the American assumption, during and immediately after World War II, that leadership of the West should automatically fall into the hands of the young, powerful, and wealthy United States.

Of the three emotions competing today in the Russian mind, humiliation is perhaps the easiest to understand. During the years 1989 to 1991, from the fall of the Berlin Wall to the dissolution of the Soviet Union, Russia lived through the equivalent of what France experienced as a result of the French Revolution and the loss of its colonial empire, though in just two years rather than a span of nearly two centuries.

First, the Russians lived through a complete reversal of their norms and values. What had been deemed wrong—capitalism, liberalism, democracy—was suddenly declared right, while socialism and communism were suddenly declared wrong. Second, Russia suffered an abrupt and shocking loss of international status. From being one of the world's two superpowers (by the 1980s even the Russians knew they were the lesser of the two), now Russia had become, at least in its own eyes, a mere card in the hands of U.S. diplomats.

Making matters worse, its state, its empire, and its army, the three key elements of its national identity, all had imploded at the same time. And unlike France and Great Britain, Russia had lost an empire that was not separated from the homeland by oceans but that lay directly on its doorstep and had been transformed overnight from a source of pride into a source of anxiety. In their newly gained independence and diplomatic and political freedom, the new countries from Georgia to Ukraine and the Baltic states were living, painful reminders of the demise of the Russian empire. When, within a few years, they sought membership in NATO, this simply sealed the sense of humiliation suffered by the Russians.

In Russia, humiliation has been accompanied by fear, a fear exacerbated by the country's xenophobic tradition, which is now being manipulated and exaggerated for political purposes. Chechnya may be seen by the Russian leadership as a military victory. On a pile of ruins and suffering, some semblance of a Russian order has been reestablished in Grozny. But the Russian triumph has been a Pyrrhic one. The Chechnya conflict has both exposed and exacerbated Russia's troubles: its widespread corruption, including that of its military forces; its reliance on unrestrained violence, spreading from Chechnya to the rest of the country; its leaders' flawed priorities, focused on reinforcing the power of the state rather than the well-being of its citizens; and, ultimately, its failure to become a "normal," civilized country in which the rule of law is paramount.

Yet in today's Russia, humiliation and fear are also accompanied by the spectacular reappearance of hope, hope in its most materialistic form. If most Russians feel better today than they did five or ten years ago, it is because Russia looks better, because living conditions are steadily improving, and because the economy was growing at an annual rate of around 7 percent per year. This has nothing to do with the exhilarating spiritual and ideological hope of the early revolutionary years, right after 1917. Today's Russian hope is, ironically, highly Marxist in the sense that it is driven mainly by economic factors. (It wasn't Marx who said, "It's the economy, stupid," but it could have been.) This materialism is accompanied by nationalism and a renewed sense of pride, which is manifested particularly in sports, from soccer to the Olympic Games.

And if the resurgence of the economy has been accompanied by a crackdown on civil society and a return to autocracy, what of it? The Russians never based their sense of self-worth or national pride on their ability to maintain a Western-style democracy. In fact, the latter part of the Gorbachev era and the Yeltsin years that followed, which saw the emergence of something like a civil society coupled with a weak democratic impulse, were viewed by most Russians as a time of humiliation. Democracy was, if anything, a sign of weakness in the eyes of a population that had lost its empire, had lost its international status, and viewed even the pitiable physical condition of its leader and his visible lack of dignity as daily humiliations.

Putin understood all this. The undeniable sense of progress and even hope he has helped re-create, along with a sense of recovered status, was of course greatly helped by the increase in gas and oil prices to new levels that are likely to remain high for the foreseeable future. Where will hope be in Russia when the price of a barrel of oil is closer to $40 rather than $150? But despite the fluctuations in the price of oil, the Russian reserves are priceless, and most Russians are thrilled that "Russia is back." They don't care about the fact that Russia's return seems to mean a further deepening of the gap between Russia and the West (in terms at least of political culture) and a rapprochement between Russia and Asia (meaning a drift toward "Oriental despotism" and away from democracy).

At the same time, the drift toward autocracy doesn't mean that one can simply dismiss the March 2008 election in which Medvedev was enthroned as Putin's successor as a mere farce. It was not a democratic election in the Western sense of the term—that is, marked by free competition and equal access to both the ballot and the media. Its result nevertheless corresponded to the wishes of the majority of Russians. And in his first public statements after being elected, Medvedev emphasized the need for the rule of law in Russia, a reassuring intention that has yet to be translated into reality but is a meaningful signal nonetheless.

It is tempting to draw parallels between Russia and another great regional power, Iran.

Both Russia and Iran know that at the moment their key source of power and influence is their energy wealth. Both feel confident, rightly or wrongly, that time is working in their favor. Both have experienced humiliation in their recent histories (with the American-led overthrow of Prime Minister Mossadegh in 1953 as Iran's equivalent of the collapse of the Soviet Union), and both use humiliation in their discourse as a propaganda weapon, a source of anger and a rallying cry. The common message shared by the leadership of both countries is: "You'll never fool us and humiliate us again as you did yesterday." In the war in Georgia in the summer of 2008, the Russian message to the West was "You fear me, therefore I exist."

But there is one major difference between Russia and Iran. Russia is an aging country with a male population decimated by the abuse of vodka and a bad health system, a demography that is in total contrast with the youthful, entrepreneurial, and hopeful spirit that characterizes the "new Russian" business leaders—or did before the economic crisis of 2008.

By contrast, Iran is a young country whose striving, open energy has nothing to do with the profoundly anachronistic nature of the "bearded clerics" who lead it. In this context, the eccentric obsessions of Iran's ruling class, such as President Ahmadinejad's frequent invocations of the inevitable collapse of the "Zionist entity," appear both as an attempt to court the Arab street and as a desperate effort to obscure or paper over the government's growing political fragility and unpopularity.

ISRAEL: FROM HOPE TO ANGST

The state of Israel is another strategically important country that defies easy classification in terms of emotions. As in Russia, there is a combination of fear, hope, and humiliation. It may seem strange that a large old empire and a small, very young state should exhibit similar identity problems. But both countries have a difficult, ambiguous relationship with Europe, and both exhibit an intense sense of vulnerability based on a sense of being encircled by hostile forces even as they boast of being the unrivaled economic and military powers of their regions.

The fear in Israel is based on several factors. One is demography. Jewish Israelis are simply too few in comparison with the Arabs, whose rate of population growth means that unless boundary lines are soon redrawn, Israel is bound to become a majority Arab nation. On a broader scale, when we compare the numbers of Jews and Muslims in the world, as the Jews of Israel undoubtedly do, we can't help seeing the Jews as a tiny, vulnerable group pitted against a vast and rapidly growing collection of a billion people spread out over dozens of nations, most of them actually or potentially hostile to Israel.

Combine these demographic factors with the local political violence and regional strategic threats that Israel faces, and the fear Israelis experience isn't difficult to understand. The second intifada was a fundamental mistake for the Palestinians; it ended up in a crushing defeat for them. Yet the suicide bombers did succeed in instilling fear in Israelis, almost balancing by their inhuman sacrifice the technological superiority of their adversaries and stunning the world by their willingness to turn their own bodies into weapons of absolute precision. The security wall built by Israelis between themselves and the threatening Other is the best physical incarnation of Israel's justified feeling of fear.

Fear comes also from Iran, from its support for Hezbolla and Hamas, and its combination of words and deeds, verbal provocation and nuclear ambitions. Can a country imbued with an absolutist ideology and an avowed hostility to Israel be allowed to have access to the absolute weapon? For a country that is spiritually and, to some extent, physically composed of survivors of the Holocaust and their descendants conditioned by it, this represents an unacceptable threat, not only to their homeland but to the Jewish people themselves.

Yet hope is also present in Israel in high quantity. The very creation of the country can only be seen as the triumph of hope against logic. "It is reasonable to believe in miracles," as David Ben-Gurion, the first leader of Israel, used to say. Today the incredible achievements of this new country in business, technology, science, literature, and the arts have reinforced its sense of hope. This pride offsets, at least to some degree, the national dissatisfaction with the poor quality of its political elite (as shown by the continued mishandling of the festering Palestinian problem) and, since the unfortunate war in Lebanon, with its military establishment. As many wags have said, in Israel everything goes well except the essential. In fact, one is tempted to speak of an "Italianization" of Israel, with a society more resilient than ever and a weakening state, prisoner of its electoral system of proportional voting and its more than mediocre political leaders. But Italy is in the European Union, and Israel is in the Middle East, and the difference in political and economic neighborhoods is a profound one.

Though a majority of Israelis would probably deny it, a sense of humiliation or, more precisely, resentment is also present in Jewish Israeli culture, constituting a persistent obstacle to the success of the peace process. Of course being constantly under attack by terrorist enemies who can be neither eliminated nor neutralized naturally creates a sense of helpless frustration that is closely akin to humiliation. But the emotions felt by Israelis cannot be explained by Middle East realities alone. They are also the product of Jewish history. Just as abused children often abuse their own children, the Israeli treatment of the Palestinians, blending ignorance, disdain, and brutality, may be linked to the scars the Israelis carry from the recent Jewish past. The excessive weight of history combined with a deliberate ignorance of the Other constitutes one of the most explosive emotional combinations.

AFRICA: BETWEEN DESPAIR AND HOPE

In recent decades Africa has suffered from a process of continued international marginalization exacerbated by the end of the Cold War, which took the continent off the game board as a stake in superpower rivalry. Now the ethnic violence that has recently exploded in Kenya, the African country where it was least expected, a country known for its relative prosperity and political stability, has had a profoundly negative impact on the already poor international image of the African continent. If massacres can take place there, is there any reasonable hope for the rest of the continent? This sense of foreboding has been further heightened by the tragedy of Zimbabwe, which reads more and more like a Shakespearean drama with each passing month.

Yet in spite of the prevalent impression of gloom, reinforced by the media tendency to privilege bad news over good, Africa is actually emerging, if slowly, from the deep pit of poverty and corruption into which it has fallen. More than a generation ago we witnessed the historic evils of colonialism being aggravated by the failures of decolonization and those of successive Western models of development, whether Marxist or capitalist. If today some commentators who care for Africa, like the *New York Times* columnist Nicholas Kristof, go so far as to describe it as "a land of hope," it means that behind the apparent endless despair of the African continent, positive changes can be detected. But when the rich get less rich, as is the case in 2008–2009, the poor traditionally get poorer.

But even the reasons for that change of outlook on Africa are fraught with ambivalence. Foreign investors attracted by the continent's huge energy resources and unique wealth in rare and precious materials—the Indians, the Brazilians, the Americans, and above all the Chinese desperate for energy resources— have rediscovered Africa. And because the Chinese are among the foreigners least able or willing to give lessons in "good governance" to "backward" African regimes, these often morally and financially corrupt regimes in turn find the Chinese the easiest to deal with. On both sides, greed and fear are the simple motivating factors: the Chinese fear of the absolute chaos that would cut access to Africa's unique and precious resources and the African fear of losing power without the presence of an understanding and supportive client.

Among Europeans, especially those whose countries were former colonial powers in Africa, the attitude toward Africa includes both a real concern for the future of Africans and a similar blend of greed and fear. In the European case, it is the fear of having too many Africans rushing to Europe to escape lives of misery at home. The Mediterranean Sea, no longer the "cradle of civilization" French historian Fernand Braudel described, has become a lake where the world's well-off, cruising in their yachts, can briefly glimpse the refugees from the other side of the water, clinging to their precarious craft as they risk their lives to reach the "European paradise."

French President Nicolas Sarkozy's new plan of a Union for the Mediterranean (an act to unite all EU members with several non-EU countries that border the Mediterranean) is at least in part aimed at providing an answer to this growing refugee problem. The reasoning among enlightened Europeans is simple: We have to create a future in Africa for the Africans if we want them to stay where they are.

Of course any European attempt to reform Africa must rely on the active participation of Africans. The idea that Africa, after forty years of independence, will be "saved" by Western intervention is both demeaning to the Africans and dispiriting to Westerners who want the best for Africa. It is also inaccurate. One of the most important political events of the twentieth century, the peaceful birth of majority rule in South Africa, was a transcendent moment created by the African themselves. F. W. de Klerk had the intelligence and the courage to realize before it was too late that the self-preservation of a white minority presence in South Africa required not only the end of apartheid but also the handing over of power to the black majority. Luckily, he had for partner Nelson Mandela, a man rightly celebrated as one of the greatest heroes of his time, who was animated not by a spirit of revenge but one of reconciliation. (If only the Palestinians had had their own equivalent of Mandela, rather than the weak and incompetent Arafat . . . and if only the Israeli de Klerk, Yitzhak Rabin, had not been murdered by a fanatic . . .)

Today South Africa is one nation, white and black, its unity cemented by sports events like the victories of the national team in the Rugby World Cup in 1995 and 2007 and the upcoming hosting of soccer's Mundial in 2010. South Africa's experience is a lesson for the rest of the continent: The international community can make a difference, but it cannot create or impose the conditions of peace and development.

Those conditions will require enormous changes all over the continent, including South Africa itself, where democracy is plagued by the rise of violence and corruption. The problems that Africa confronts are well known: the spread of HIV/AIDS (which affects, for example, 20 percent of the population in South Africa); the profound poverty, in which hundreds of millions remain mired; and the artificiality of boundaries inherited from the colonial period, which leads to weak feelings of national unity and the constant danger of fracturing along tribal or ethnic lines. Africa is the world's most war-torn continent by far. From Darfur to Sierra Leone, from Congo to Ivory Coast, horrifying tales of misery and murder, including the systematic use of rape as a weapon of terror and humiliation, abound. And almost everywhere, governmental corruption and incompetence blended with an ever-present fear of crime and violence are accepted as normal conditions of life.

Yet there remain reasons for hope. There is a new generation of leaders, exemplified by President Paul Kagame of Rwanda, who sees himself (with some exaggeration) as an African version of Lee Kuan Yew in Singapore, and President Ellen Johnson-Sirleaf of Liberia, benevolent autocrats ready to take the strong but humane steps necessary to bring their nations into the twenty-first century. There is the increasingly important role of women, symbolized by Kenya's Wangari Maathai (the human rights and environmental activist who won the Nobel Peace Prize in 2004), who are claiming their rightful role as the engine of hope for Africa.

There is economic hope as well. More and more countries are adopting the Botswana model, welcoming foreign investors and following the rule of markets. Aside from Rwanda, as Nicholas Kristof remarks, "countries like Mozambique, Benin, Tanzania and Mauritius are among those trying to build a future on trade more than aid." Kristof even concludes his column with an investment tip: "Buy real estate in Benin and Rwanda," a recommendation that will definitely sound too daring but that indicates the slowly shifting status of Africa. It is a continent between two worlds, poised between despair and hope, a hope that is emerging for the first time in decades, if not centuries.

If art can prefigure life, perhaps hope will win out in the end. One of the features of the 2008 London theatrical season was a South African township version of Mozart's Magic Flute, played with traditional African instruments. It radiated a joy and energy that even went beyond the universal power of Mozart's music, the spirit of Africa coming to life.

A year earlier one might have attended the Paris debut of Bintou Wéré, an Opera from the Sahel. In the last scene of the opera, a young mother who has crossed the desert to give birth to her child in a European enclave is injured by a car participating in the Paris–Dakar race. Mortally hurt, she engages in a final dialogue with the chorus over the question, Should her child be raised in Europe or in Africa? In the end she chooses Africa.

It is of course a highly symbolic decision. Africans must create hope in their own homelands, not search for it elsewhere.

LATIN AMERICA: BETWEEN DEMAGOGY AND PROGRESS

The situation of the Latin American continent is significantly different from that of Africa, even if there are common lessons to be derived from the two continents. There is less despair in Latin America but also probably less hope, with the notable exception of Brazil, the giant of the continent. Brazil likes to see itself as the China or the United States of Latin America and is convinced that its closest potential rival for that role, Mexico, is a distant second. Brazil booms with energy, dynamism, and optimism but also suffers greatly from the plagues besetting the entire continent.

Consider, for example, the plague of violence. In 2005, an average year, forty thousand people were killed by gunfire in Brazil, two thousand in Rio de Janeiro alone. Many were killed by stray bullets, simply because they happened to be in the wrong place at the wrong time. The combination of social inequality and economic dynamism may remind us of Asia, but the specter of violence gives the inequality of Brazil an especially sinister quality. The wealthy neighborhoods of Rio de Janeiro, surrounded by the notorious favelas (Portuguese for "shantytowns"), have become like fortresses protected by heavy walls, private guards, and heavily armed residents (who share the North American attitude of acceptance toward firearms).

Nonetheless, hope remains as the dominant emotion in Brazil. Even the regime of President Luiz Inácio Lula da Silva, in spite of its severe limitations—in particular Lula's "tolerance" of corruption—has a reassuring Christian trade unionist quality. Unfortunately, we can't say the same about the governments in the rest of the continent, with the exceptions of Chile (which has rediscovered its solid democratic tradition after the tragic Pinochet era). Possibly Argentina (in spite of its persistently messy economic situation), and even Colombia (where the toughness of President Álvaro Uribe in his war against the revolutionary movement of the FARC seems to be paying off).

The South American continent seems to move in cycles. When the military regimes of the 1960s proved incapable of resolving the economic crisis, they were followed in the 1980s by the return of democracy and civilian rule. Today Latin America is experiencing a populist cycle with the emergence of a new type of national leader coming from the native Indian as opposed to the Hispanic past, following a decade of extreme economic liberalism, which nearly ruined countries such as Argentina.

The figure of Hugo Chávez in Venezuela has replaced that of Fidel Castro in Cuba as the leading symbol of destabilizing left-wing influence. Chávez has both less charisma and less gravitas than Castro—in fact he can be seen as an illustration of the Marxist dictum "History repeats itself, first as tragedy, second as farce"—but at the helm of a petrostate, Chávez has one thing Castro never had: plenty of cash, even if it flows less easily these days. By buying the huge debts of countries such as Argentina, Chávez is not only making potentially huge profits but expanding his political influence in the continent.

The cycle of populism in Latin America is less a function of hope than of humiliation. Whereas the people of India have largely solved their problems with their former colonial power, Great Britain, this is far from being the case in Latin America, where relations with the North American gringos (as well as with Spain, the former colonial power) remain both central and difficult.

Of course the United States bears the major responsibility for this psychological and political condition. The United States seems to continue to apply toward its Latin American "backyard" (itself a condescending term) the same attitude it severely denounced when it was applied by European powers to their former African colonies. Although U.S. interventions are now usually indirect, America remains both a vital balancer and a resented source of outside interference throughout Latin America.

Beyond humiliation there is also fear, but, again, curiously intermixed with contrasting emotions. Weak states, if not failed states, abound in Latin America as in Africa. Drug cartels dispute the state's monopoly on the legitimate use of violence. Civil wars drag on for decades in countries such as Colombia, even if Bogotá is actually safer than most big Brazilian cities. And to judge by growth rates alone, one must speak of something like a Colombian economic miracle. Armed with powerful cash flows, petrostates like Venezuela behave like regional energy superpowers, striving to balance the American and Brazilian influences on the continent while also expressing a kind of populist native American-Indian rebellion against national elites.

In the beginning of the twenty-first century, the jury is still out on Africa and Latin America. Policy makers, businesspeople, and those concerned with human development cannot ignore these two continents. But they are not, not yet, the places where the future of the world is being decided, nor will they become so in the foreseeable future.

Chapter Six

THE WORLD IN 2025

My attempt to use emotions as a way of deciphering the world and the collective behavior of nations will make this book heretical in the eyes of most political scientists and international relations specialists. To add insult to injury, let me now go even further and engage in an exercise of historical fantasy, aimed at developing a citizen's reflexes.

The world I have endeavored to analyze through the prism of emotions is the world we live in, a world that is both dangerous and exciting. And what of the future? The world can go either way, for if the very best is unlikely, the worst is not inevitable either. The intended message of this concluding chapter can be summarized very simply: "You have your destiny in your hands. Choose!"

With this in mind, let's consider how our world might look if fear were to come to dominate it or, conversely, if hope were to rule. The two scenarios I am going to present are of course caricatures. The reality is likely to be somewhere in between.

Regarding the negative scenario: Cassandras are necessary because they give wake-up calls. But they may also become dangerous if they are invoked in order to foster a culture of fear. That is not my intention. I hope you will read my forecast for a world in which fear has triumphed as a cautionary story, illustrating what may happen to us if we make the mistake of allowing negative emotions to overrule our judgment.

As for the hopeful scenario, I am realistic enough to know that it is just a dream that will not materialize in exactly the form I depict. But even dreaming has its purpose. An enlightened dream indicates the direction the world could take under the guidance of the right leaders, armed with the right principles and having at their disposal the right institutional mechanisms—along with a bit of luck. Such a dream can serve as an enticement to do better, to work harder for a better world.

FEAR PREVAILS

It is November 2025. In Tel Aviv, Israel is observing the thirtieth anniversary of the assassination of Yitzhak Rabin in an atmosphere of gloom and foreboding. Since the start of the fourth intifada in 2018, the security conditions have worsened again, not only in Israel and Palestine but throughout the Middle East. One result has been the gradual decline of both Jewish and Arab populations in Israel, as everyone with an alternative place to live has been fleeing, trying to escape not only the atmosphere of violence but the oppressive conditions imposed by life in a state of near-martial law.

Unfortunately, Israel is not the only place where an obsession with security is making life less rewarding. In fact a certain "Israelization" of life around the world has become a reality. The culture of fear is now practically universal, especially after the successful use of biological weapons by terrorist networks in San Francisco, London, Paris, Prague, Tokyo, Mumbai, and several other European and Asian cities during the infamous "White Death" attacks of 2019–2020. In the wake of those attacks, which killed some thirty thousand people, most governments have instituted harsh security measures. Borders have been shut down, national ID cards are required for virtually any economic activity, dissident groups (even nonviolent ones) have been banned and their leaders arrested, and everyday life involves a gauntlet of military checkpoints, physical searches, and other inconveniences that keep millions of people in a constant state of tension, frustration, and anxiety.

There is of course no global referee or peacekeeper to channel or coordinate the international response to the terrorist threat, the United Nations and its sister institutions having fallen into disuse after multiple failed attempts at self-reformation. Multilateralism is dead, and with it the hope of a world of unity and stability based on consensus and the rule of law.

Some had hoped that the United States would be able to fill the leadership void left by the demise of multilateral institutions. Unfortunately, despite the election of a Democratic president in 2008 and the subsequent attempt to shift the nation's course, the United States had neither the ability nor the will to do to so. Financially, militarily, and psychologically depleted by ruinous wars in the Middle East and the devastating recession of 2008–2014, the United States retreated into a neoprotectionist shell, withdrawing most forces from foreign soil and, more damagingly, sharply reducing its involvement in international diplomacy and problem solving as well. The shift was confirmed in 2013, when the newly elected president, a far-right-wing conservative with strongly jingoist and protectionist policies, announced a dramatic reduction in U.S. armed forces, with the remaining soldiers to be deployed almost exclusively along the now heavily fortified borders with Mexico and Canada.

In retrospect, this American retreat was perhaps inevitable. Disappointed with their failures on the world stage and their economic struggles following the financial collapse of 2008, Americans began to search obsessively for an explanation of what went wrong and even to question their own national identity. Paul Kennedy's vision of the decline of the American empire was premature when he published it in 1987. It has become a reality in 2025. As a result, a weakened America no longer has either the hard or the soft power to be the indispensable nation it has been since 1941.

The other Western powers are suffering their own psychological and emotional breakdowns. In Europe, the fears of "Balkanization" that many expressed in the 1990s during the dismantling of Yugoslavia have slowly become reality. It's difficult to say exactly what provoked the dramatic unraveling of the European Union ideal. Perhaps it was the new explosion of violence in the Balkans in 2015 over the issue of Kosovo, which demonstrated yet again the impotence of the European Union. Perhaps it was the peaceful but stunning explosion of Belgium in 2010 or the subsequent declarations of independence by Scotland, Wales, and Catalonia. Whatever the precise causes, the result is clear. Having evoked so carelessly the emotions of nationalism and economic self-determination, the leaders of Europe found themselves incapable of controlling the forces they had unleashed. What looked initially like merely the victory of a British vision of Europe, a loose, decentralized federation rather than a unified power, ended in the final defeat and near dissolution of the European Union.

In the irresistible process of divorce between the European Union and its citizens, foreshadowed by the triple no of the French, the Dutch, and the Irish to the referendums on the constitutional treaty, Europe's institutions, the commission in particular, played their part. They became prisoners of themselves, increasingly failing to relate to the feelings and demands of society in a world shaken by the depths of economic recession. As a result, European societies have tended increasingly to see Europe as part of the problem rather than part of the solution.

So far war has not returned to the heart of "Old Europe," but it threatens the continent's periphery, from the Balkans and the Caucasus to the Strait of Gibraltar. Europe has been reduced to a kind of Magna Helvetia, a giant Switzerland, still peaceful and relatively prosperous, but bereft of youthful energy (having sealed its boundaries to badly needed immigrants), militarily impotent, selfish, and largely irrelevant, a museum of its own past dominated by fear and surrounded by a sense of danger. Having given up on the idea of being a strategic and diplomatic power on the world scene, Europe is no longer a model, or if it is, it is a model of impotence.

One of Europe's main fears comes from its highly populated and unstable neighbor, Turkey. Having realized that Europe did not want them in their "Christian club," the Turks looked for alternatives. Torn between the idea of a return to some kind of neo-Ottoman glory and the temptation of a radicalized form of

Islam, Turkey is now on the verge of implosion, a full-fledged Middle Eastern country that is infecting Europe with the ethnic and religious hatreds of that region. As for Russia, it is now perceived just as it was during the Cold War: as a threat. Ukraine and Georgia remain formally independent (unlike Belorussia, which has been reabsorbed into the Russian empire), but the orders issued by puppet governments in Kiev and Tbilisi are written in Moscow.

Yet the fate of Europe still looks enviable compared with that of other continents.

Asia was the continent of hope in the early years of the twenty-first century. Now it is returning to be what it was in the 1950s and 1960s, the continent of war.

The process began of course with the costly and irresponsible war launched by China on Taiwan in 2014. It was driven by internal factors. The brutal cessation of Chinese economic growth, combined with devastating environmental problems, led to a deep social crisis and violent political upheaval. In desperation, Beijing's Communist leaders played the nationalist card, their weapon of last resort for retaining power. Taiwan's careless use of independence rhetoric and symbols gave Beijing an ideal pretext for the invasion of that small island. The United States refused to intervene directly, but its military help to Taiwan made the war much longer and more difficult than the Chinese had expected.

Now the Middle Empire is finally reunited, but at what cost? China's period of economic growth is over. Having failed to reform themselves politically, China and India have fallen back on nationalistic rhetoric to divert their citizens' attention from the shortcomings of their governments and from the hunger riots that have regularly exploded in the two countries, making their food situation terribly similar to that of the African continent. The climate of tension that now exists between China and India as a result of their mounting internal tensions could well break into open war between two nuclear giants, without the technical and cultural restraints that the Cold War exerted on the United States and the Soviet Union. The demography of the two Asian giants is such that they both are flirting recklessly—to be

fair, the undemocratic Chinese much more than the Indians—
with the idea of risking the lives of "only" a few hundred million people for the sake of national glory.

In reaction, almost all Asia is in arms: Cambodians versus
Thais, Vietnamese versus Cambodians. . . . Caught between the
existence of a fundamentalist Taliban-like regime armed with
nuclear weapons in Pakistan and the strongly nationalistic and
aggressive behavior of China and India, the Japanese have shed
their historical aversion to military might and have joined the
growing club of Asian nuclear powers. The shifting balance of
terror in Asia is proving to be anything but a source of stability for the region. In fact it is threatening economic growth,
making the continent too risky for the tastes of international
investors.

The Asian culture of hope has been further eroded by environmental degradation and the destabilizing effects of extreme
religious ideology. Uncontrolled economic development and its
ecological consequences have helped create a legitimate culture
of fear in Asia thanks to the sharp increases in the severity and
frequency of tsunamis, floods, typhoons, and landslides, along
with the escalating health costs of uncontrolled pollution. At
the same time, a growing "Arabization" of Asian Islam has led
to a further radicalization of Hindu fundamentalists, helping
spread a climate of religious intolerance all over Asia. Now even
countries like Singapore have lost their magic touch, with the
relationships of various communities (such as Chinese and Indians) becoming a serious source of internal tension.

With the West in disarray and Asia having exchanged hope
for fear, the African continent has fallen prey to despair, de-
population, and ethnic warfare. The Chinese, the Indians, the
Americans, and the Europeans, preoccupied with their own
problems, have abandoned Africa. Left to their own fate, the
Africans have returned to the practices and behavior that led to
earlier failures. Infectious diseases are endemic, poverty rates
have resumed their upward climb, and governmental corruption is as rampant as ever.

Even the experience of postapartheid South Africa has turned
sour. With the uncontrollable escalation of violence, a majority

of the white community has left the country, mainly for Australia and New Zealand. What is the meaning of reconciliation if it is not accompanied by peace and hope for the future?

Latin America is yet another victim of the chaotic state of the world. Brazil and Mexico, the continent's two giants, both have suffered as a result of their respective strategies for development. Having chosen to align itself with the United States through NAFTA, Mexico has been hit hard by the American crisis of confidence and its escalating protectionist and neo-isolationist policies. As for Brazil, which chose a globalized economic strategy at least in part as an act of defiance toward the United States, it has been weakened by the partial withdrawal of China and India from world markets as a result of their internal struggles and their preoccupation with military confrontation.

The only real winner in Latin America is the spirit of populism, in its various forms from "post-Peronism" to "post-Castroism." Military institutions have reclaimed a major political role in several Latin American countries, sometimes sharing control with drug cartels that are more powerful than ever.

Each of these disheartening regional trends has had its own causes. But is there any overarching force to which we can point as a driver of the global collapse of the last twenty years?

If there is, perhaps we can summarize it this way: *The clash of civilizations has changed from a provocative intellectual construct into a self-fulfilling prophecy.*

When Samuel Huntington first articulated his tragic notion of an inevitable clash between Islam and the West in 1993, it seemed to many to be exaggerated and even a little hysterical. But in the years that followed, a series of almost irresistible processes turned it into reality. The terror attacks of 9/11 were not the cause, but they certainly helped accelerate a cascade of events, including misunderstandings, miscalculations, and misjudgments, that led us to the current sad state of affairs. Throughout it all, the fear that Huntington's vision was correct has been one of the forces promoting the growth of chaos, largely outside the consciousness of the people making the decisions. "Men make history, but they do not know the history they are making," as the German philosopher Hegel wrote.

The tipping point, perhaps, was the American and Israeli air attacks on Iran that led to the overthrow of Ahmadinejad. Technically the attacks were a success, but like the war in Iraq, they were a political catastrophe, producing an explosion of anti-Western hatred in the entire Muslim world.

The first victim of this emotional escalation was democracy in Pakistan. The democratic process Pervez Musharraf suspended so many times was too weak to prevent the rise of a jihadi regime that inherited Pakistan's nuclear arsenal. The inevitable consequence was a nuclear proliferation race in the Middle East. Confronted with the threat of nuclear fundamentalism, Saudi Arabia, Egypt, and Turkey all turned nuclear.

In response, the West turned itself into a fortress, rejecting both people and ideas from the Middle East as well as manufactured goods coming from Asia. Immigrant communities throughout Europe found themselves under attack, subject both to armed violence from local natives and to harassment by government authorities. By 2018 roundups and deportations of tens of thousands of foreigners had begun all over Europe, paralleling the similar roundups of Latin Americans that had swept the United States five years earlier. Everywhere, it seems, the Other has become a source of suspicion and fear in the new antiglobalization atmosphere that prevails.

In cultural terms, we are no longer living in the hopeful world of Beethoven; we have moved to the tragic, barbaric beauty of the last works of Wagner. But if the world of 2025 sounds like Wagner, it looks like a cartoon by the Serbo-French artist Enki Bilal (creator of violent, apocalyptic fantasies), a movie like *Blade Runner*, or a scene from one of Shakespeare's most violent plays (such as *Titus Andronicus*), depicting a world of fury and dark disorder.

The global situation now resembles that of the early Middle Ages in Europe following the collapse of the Roman Empire, when the barbarians took center stage and ushered in a period of violence, chaos, and turmoil. Those "Dark Ages" lasted almost half a millennium. How long will these new Dark Ages persist? No one can say.

HOPE PREVAILS

It is November 2025. Here in Tel Aviv, on the square that now carries his name, Yitzhak Rabin was assassinated exactly thirty years ago. Today this city is the site of a major international celebration to commemorate the fifth anniversary of the Middle Eastern peace treaty that finally brought to an end more than seventy years of violence, insecurity, and injustice. Representatives of all the members of the enlarged Security Council of the United Nations are present, including the United States, China, India, Russia, Brazil, and South Africa. Of course the recently united European Union is now represented by a single envoy.

As one looks back on the successful conclusion of the Middle East talks five years earlier, it still appears a remarkable achievement. The truth is that after so many decades of conflict, no one really expected a breakthrough for peace. Perhaps the resolution, when it came, was the result of fatigue as much as any yearning for peace. Israelis and Palestinians had come to the conclusion that they needed each other to survive (in the case of Israel) or simply to exist (in the case of the Palestinians).

One by one, the necessary emotional building blocks for peace fell into place. The Muslim nations had realized that the fate of the Palestinians—in their eyes, an obscure local group toward which they had never really felt any profound loyalty—had become a dangerous fixation that was needlessly preventing progress. The Israelis had come to accept the reality that the Palestinians were a permanent part of the landscape of their homeland. "Paris is well worth a mass," as Henri IV famously remarked; in the same vein, Israelis now declared, "Peace is well worth surrendering part of Jerusalem and the territories." And when the Palestinians abandoned their claim that refugees must have the right of return, shifting, in effect, from a culture of absolutism to a culture of compromise, the outlines of a practical settlement were suddenly clear, and peace was, stunningly, around the corner.

Equally important, perhaps, was the transformation of the

international environment into one where the forces that opposed peace were suddenly weaker than those that favored it, an environment in which the absence of peace between Israelis and Palestinians looked anachronistic. The power most responsible for this transformation of the international environment was the United States.

In truth a culture of hope has always come more naturally to the people of America than has a culture of fear. So perhaps it should not have come as a great surprise when following the watershed election of 2008, the United States began to recover confidence in itself after the moral trauma of the war in Iraq. Within a few years America had largely regained its unique soft power as the most widely respected country on earth.

In large part, this turnabout happened because the leadership of the United States decided to accept gracefully its nation's relative decline in classical power terms. ("Relative" only, of course; the United States remained the most powerful nation on the planet.) The superpower of the Cold War and the hyperpower of the post–Cold War years resigned itself to being simply one nation among all the others, even if a slightly more powerful one. Given the painful impact of its last imperial adventure on American society and the American economy, not to mention on the image of America in the world, this "sacrifice" felt much less traumatic to Americans themselves than most commentators had expected. And in the wake of the financial trauma of 2008, many Americans were ready to accept a call to rebuild their nation's economy and infrastructure rather than squander scarce resources in further adventures overseas.

Freed from their self-imposed mission to transform the world through the exporting of democracy, Americans turned to the cause of protecting the environment with a passion explicable only by the Puritan streak in American culture. Having ratified an amended version of the Tokyo protocol, America became the world's leading advocate of green policies. By 2015 amended auto emissions standards, a carbon cap and trade program, new hybrid and electric cars, and strict new policies on air pollution had begun an absolute decline in the production of greenhouse gases by the United States. Not incidentally, the new industries spurred by these technological innovations created millions of new jobs for Americans and helped make the recession of 2008–2010 both less severe and less prolonged than most economists had predicted.

In a broader sense, America's attitude toward the world had changed. There was a run on passport offices as Americans took up international travel with greater enthusiasm than ever. Encouraged by a president with multicultural roots and interests, Americans began studying the cultures and languages of other countries. Real curiosity and even empathy gradually replaced the mixture of ignorance and disdain that had once characterized Americans abroad. In return, the world began again to appreciate and value those qualities that had always made America unique: its commitment to democracy; its spirit of openness, tolerance, innovation, and freedom—in sum, a real and positive universalism.

Having survived the twin dangers of imperial hubris and neo-isolationism, the United States remained engaged in the affairs of the world, now appearing as a senior partner but no longer as the unique arbiter and policeman of the world. As a result, its international image improved considerably. The anti-American culture that had become such a popular rallying point for a Europe in search of its identity receded.

During the decades of the 2010s a series of American leaders presided over the "reconciliation" between the United States and the United Nations. Americans had come to realize the need for a strong and legitimate international referee in an age of complexity and interdependency. Only the UN could play that role, strengthened by its new, more broadly representative Security Council and a dynamic, charismatic new secretary-general. Supported by the United States, the new secretary-general had at her disposal both a streamlined UN bureaucracy and a strong military force. These "mercenaries of peace," made up mostly of Gurkha regiments from Nepal (with their well-known reputation for toughness and discipline), were able to exert a powerful deterrent effect on would-be aggressors as well as on leaders tempted to use force against their own people. Wisely applied, the duty to interfere doctrine had survived its unfortunate misuse during the war in Iraq and became a basic foundation of the new international legal system.

As important as the renaissance of the UN were the gradual emergence and acceptance of a new multipolar order, bringing relative stability to the world scene. For Europeans, this was simply a return to normalcy, for such an equilibrium of power had been in place in Europe from the mid-seventeenth century to the first half of the twentieth century. Unlike the older European case, the new informal "council of great powers" was not united by monarchical principles, nor was it the great alliance of democracies proposed by some Americans in the early 2000s. Yet it was a homogeneous, reasonable coherent order, because the key participants were united by a single principle to which they all adhered—the rule of law as administered primarily by the shared referee of the United Nations—as well as a common concern for the ecological well-being of the planet and the absolute need to meet successfully the challenge of global warming. The International Tribunal of The Hague now plays a vital, fully recognized role as the guarantor of universal rights and legal principles.

Of course, within the broad sweep of the new council, there were genuine differences of ideology and interest. Europe and the United States shared a common culture based on democratic principles. India, as the great Asian democracy, constituted a bridge between the West and the other leading powers, China and Russia, which, while not on the path to democracy, had nonetheless come to see the value to them of supporting a system based on the rule of law, domestically as well as internationally. The slow opening of the Chinese regime to a new generation of leaders free of personal ties to the Communist past had opened the way to incremental imposition in China of the rule of law on the model of Singapore. After nearly twenty years under Putin, directly or indirectly, Russia too had moved toward accepting the rule of law, mainly in order to maintain its business credibility and competitiveness.

Eager to balance its giant Chinese neighbor, Russia had come to the conclusion that its future was with the West. Accordingly, it had formed with the European Union an informal "club," acting in concert on most major issues and working out economic problems in a basically cooperative spirit. This Union for a Greater Europe had managed to create a new climate of confidence between Russia and its European neighbors, including those like Poland that were once controlled by it. And Ukraine, now a member of the union, acts as a perfect bridge between Russia and the rest of Europe, just as Poland did fifteen years earlier.

As for the European Union itself, it evolved according to a vision quite distinct from that of its founding fathers. By 2020 Europe had become not merely a civilian power or a purely economic force but also a limited military force to be reckoned with within the framework of a revitalized and rebalanced Atlantic Alliance. This evolution was made possible by the return of France into NATO in 2009. It was a European force within the NATO structure that guaranteed the implementation of the Israeli-Palestinian peace treaty, a natural development, since it was only right that Europe, which had been part of the origin of the Middle Eastern problem (through colonialism and the Holocaust), should be part of its solution.

In the reawakening of the European Union, three factors were decisive. First, the union's attractiveness as a model remained high, as evidenced by the continuing interest in joining the union by countries on its periphery. By 2016 the former Yugoslavia was a member of the union, its "exploded" multiple sovereignties and identities having been de facto reunited under the roof of the union. After Croatia in 2010, Serbia, Kosovo, and Montenegro had jointly entered the union, followed shortly by Macedonia and Bosnia and even Albania. Thus Europe's peace and prosperity prevailed over the specter of the return of war to the Balkans. Justice had proved decisive in this process of further enlargement of the union, as the arrest of war criminals and the well-reasoned judgments pronounced in The Hague had paved the way to the reconciliation of the entire European continent with itself.

In a further demonstration of the ongoing allure of Europe, Turkey will join the union later in 2025. The progress of the Turkish economy and the stability of its democratic institutions have impressed otherwise reluctant Europeans, encouraged by the new climate of détente between Islam and the West, that the time has come to transcend the prejudices of the past and the diktat of geography.

The second crucial factor in the reawakening of Europe was the relaunching of the European institutional process following the signing of the revised European treaty in 2010. Europeans have a new president, a defense minister, a foreign minister, and a diplomatic service. It was only a matter of time before these developments would lead to the unenthusiastic but wise agreement by France and Great Britain to give up their individual seats in the UN Security Council in favor of a single European representative.

The third factor was of a more moral and psychological nature. At the same time that Americans were learning to be more modest in accepting the new multipolar world, Europeans were recovering the sense of energy and ambition they had lost during and after the Cold War years. The time for European (and even Western) supremacy was gone, but Europe could still play an important role on the world stage. Europeans sensed that it was time to outgrow the historical fatigue they'd suffered after the great wars of the twentieth century. Now, with their societies renewed through the arrival of new immigrants, the integration of influences from new member countries, and the growing assertiveness of women, Europeans were ready to drop their fascination with decay, their growing cynicism about themselves and the world, and their collective escapism. Today, at last, Europe is back.

Of course the current roster of five leading world powers—the United States, China, India, Russia, and the European Union—is not permanent. In the near future, other forces, including Brazil, South Africa, and the newly reunited republic of Korea, will have to be reckoned with. Japan too remains a potent economic and, more recently, political and diplomatic force.

Then there is Africa. The turning point in Africa's transition from despair to hope was first the election of Barack Obama in the United States, followed by the success of the Soccer World Cup tournament in South Africa in 2010, the psychological equivalent for the entire African continent of the 2008 Olympics for China: the international confirmation of its new status as a place and a people that matter. Having abandoned their fascination with foreign models, their dream of finding a new life in Europe, and their long-standing tendency to blame and rely on others, a new generation of African leaders decided to take their fate into their own hands.

In this dramatic shift of attitude, the Chinese investors played a major role. Their combination of interest and greed convinced Africans that if they did not want their future to be decided by others once again, they had to plan it for themselves. With help from Chinese, Indian, and Japanese technology but guided by African leaders, the continent gradually became the planet's greatest locus of economic growth and opportunity. When scientists achieved a series of breakthroughs in the treatment of HIV/AIDS, including the long-sought vaccine announced in 2011, health and life expectancies in Africa began to shoot upward. By 2018 malaria had joined smallpox on the list of infectious diseases found only in scientific laboratories.

As for Latin America, it is following the lead of Brazil and Argentina in creating the Southern Hemisphere's equivalent of the European Union. Mercosur, launched in 1991 as a regional trade association, has become a full-fledged political entity. Now called the Latin American Union, its common police and common justice system are making real progress in defeating the various drug and leftist cartels that have imposed their own will on so many countries of the continent for so long.

All these positive changes in the international climate undoubtedly helped pave the way for the Palestinian-Israeli peace accord. But there were specific regional developments that played an important role as well.

One of the most symbolic shifts took place in Lebanon, where the logic of collective prosperity replaced the logic of violence and division. The reintegration of Syria in the community of nations, after Damascus, encouraged by the United States and the European Union, decided to follow the example of Tripoli, played a major role in the emergence of a new political formula for a reinvented Lebanon. Within twelve months, Lebanon, Israel, Palestine, Syria, and Jordan signed a customs union agreement, which many observers see as the embryo of a Middle Eastern Common Market, resembling the earlier phases of the European Union, and which is an important subcomponent of the Union for the Mediterranean launched by French president Sarkozy in 2008.

There were other hopeful developments in the region as well. After the departure of the United States and its allies from Iraq and the reinforcement of troops in Afghanistan during the years 2009–2010, the stability in the two countries grew significantly. The new and responsible diplomacy of Tehran following the electoral humiliation of Ahmadinejad of course was instrumental in these positive developments, as the self-isolation to which Ahmadinejad had condemned his own country was wisely rejected by most of the Iranian people. The remarkable Asian-like economic success of the Gulf emirates benefited the entire region. The wise investments made by those states in education, banking, and renewable energy, not to mention culture, helped transform the regional environment. By consolidating the social equilibrium of giants like Egypt, they had in fact contributed more than any other outside forces to the development of the logic of peace in the Middle East and served as living proof that Islam and modernity were compatible. They were also the best answer to al Qaeda, as they helped organize and finance the resistance of moderate Islam against fundamentalism.

Within a decade, the fundamentalists were everywhere on the defensive; their time had gone. For the vast majority of Muslims, the attractiveness of martyrdom had disappeared, much as the intense appeal of anarchism and nihilism to Europeans in the late nineteenth and early twentieth centuries ultimately vanished.

In sum, we can now see that despite—or perhaps because of—the economic crisis, which forced badly needed reforms, the period beginning around 2009 was the start of a hopeful time in human history—not the "end of history" overoptimistically announced by Francis Fukuyama in 1991, but, more modestly and realistically, the return of a cycle of enlightenment. How long will it last? Will new causes of hatred and violence find their ways to the surface of human society? If so, how will the leaders of the world respond? Questions like these are ever present. But for now we can appreciate the fact that historical circumstances have conspired to usher in an epoch of hope. While we can, let's make the most of it.

What Is to Be Done?

It is likely that some of the developments fantasized in the two scenarios I just outlined will actually occur. Most won't— fortunately in the case of the first scenario, unfortunately for the second. These largely artificial tales were written with one key question in mind. If collective entities like cultures and nations can be analyzed through the prisms of psychology and emotions, is it possible to conceive of a "prescription for the world" analogous to the medical treatment that might be prescribed for an individual? Can a collective state of melancholia, depression, hysteria, or paranoia be alleviated like similar conditions in individual patients?

In 1800 the physician Marie-François-Xavier Bichat, sometimes called the founder of descriptive anatomy, defined life as the "ensemble of functions that resist death." Similarly, perhaps, we can define peace as the ensemble of functions, including emotions, that resist war and violence. There are concepts, ways of thinking and feeling, that can do much to make international strife less likely. Ideas like the duty to intervene, the idea of an international tribunal for crimes against humanity, the emphasis on "human security" beyond "national security": All these developments are part of what could be described as humanitarian deterrence, a form of preventive medicine for the international system. Their message to would-be transgressors is very clear: "National sovereignty will no longer protect you. You are accountable to the world community for your crimes."

Of course this is a generous but somewhat dangerous logic. To make it work requires conditions that are far from being met today. What would it take to create these conditions? In other words, what are the political strategies and institutional mechanisms necessary to reinforce hope and to contain or reduce fear and humiliation?

SELF-PRESERVATION MEANS CHANGE

To remain faithful to themselves and the fulfillment of their ambitions, nations and peoples that hope to play a significant role on the international stage have to accept change and to recognize that the status quo is untenable.

In Giuseppe di Lampedusa's celebrated novel *The Leopard*, Prince Salinas watches the arrival of new elites at the ball that concludes the book (a scene immortalized by its cinematic rendering), noting with a mixture of cynicism and nostalgia that "everything had to change so that everything could remain the same." The warning that I am offering is just the opposite. Things have to change quite radically if we do not want to see the international order collapse into a profound and dangerous unbalance. And national leaders themselves have to be convinced that the status quo is a recipe for disaster.

This diagnosis is in some cases simply a question of self-preservation and collective survival. As noted earlier in this book, it is the same instinct that led President de Klerk of South Africa to end apartheid.

In a less dramatic but equally imperative way, most nations and cultures have to change in order to keep hope and to transcend fear and humiliation. In Asia, for example, change means a newfound respect for the rule of law and the integration of the poorest into mainstream society. To continue to incarnate the culture of hope, China and India do not want to see economic growth rocked by the inevitable social and political instability that will result from clinging hopelessly to the status quo. Even Singapore has to change and accept fresh air and a spirit of openness if it wants to continue to attract the regional and international elites it badly needs.

As for Russia, it cannot accept passively the fatality of "Oriental despotism" in one form or another. Russians deserve better, and at some point they must set for themselves as a primary task the goal of reducing the gap between the quality of their artistic and literary culture and the poverty of their political culture.

For Russia too the continuation of the status quo in politics is a guarantee of decay.

Self-preservation in the case of the West means recovering the sense of universal values. We like to preach the superiority of our democratic model and the unique nature of our social system of protection as compared with China or even India. But are we truly practicing these values at home? Let's ask the question and take the answer seriously, disturbing though it may be.

Beyond this, self-preservation means different things for America and Europe. For America, it means regaining a sense of modesty on the world stage without falling into isolationism. It means accepting that you can become merely one "indispensable nation" among others. It means realizing that in terms of both hard and soft power, America will no longer be alone.

This message has clear and direct consequences. America has to learn to deal in a balanced way with others who are or are becoming equals, just as Europe did for most of its modern history within the framework of its balance of power system. This in turn implies understanding and accepting the cultural differences of other nations. For a long time to come, nothing in the world will be possible without America, but ever more even than in the past, nothing will be possible for America alone.

To remain faithful to its democratic essence, the American Republic has to accept this change and diminution of its international status. Imperial hubris nearly destroyed the Republic. A more modest and honest America abroad and one much more ambitious at home in social and environmental terms can reconquer its international image by recognizing that less is more and that influence and power are not the same. In other words, less power may mean more influence.

For Europe, self-preservation and change mean recovering the ambition to be a global player while retaining a primary concern for norms and models. Can the European Union become an attractive reality for its citizens and not remain a purely rational and largely dehumanized bureaucratic entity? I think so. The purpose of the European project should be to reinvent the concept of sovereignty for the twenty-first century.

Europe is no longer the center of world history. Accepting change for it is to recognize this reality, not as a tragic fatality but as a simple fact of history. Energy and hope in Europe will first come from those with the greatest appetite, the new countries, the new immigrants, and, above all, the newly empowered women. Could the twenty-first century be not only "the century of Asia" and "the century of identity" but also "the century of women"?

For the United States and Europe, the "audacity of hope" (to use Barack Obama's words) must progressively replace the "facility of fear." To make this happen, a renewed confidence in the values and mission of the West is essential.

The rise of spring for Asia does not necessarily imply the West's decline into a dark winter. A rich and mature fall is available to us, if three conditions are met. The first is that we recognize that the era of our supremacy has gone. The second is that we accept and learn from the success of others. The third, and perhaps the most important, is that we remain faithful to our values. Our difference lies in our unique brand of universalism, our deeply ingrained respect for the rule of law, and our concern for social and economic balances. If we combine this new modesty and this renewed confidence in our values, then everything remains possible, and the autumn of the West need not be synonymous with the decline of the West.

It is precisely confidence that the Arab-Islamic world needs most in order to transcend its culture of humiliation. For countries like Egypt and Saudi Arabia, any attempt to preserve the status quo would be a recipe for disaster. The remarkable success of the small Gulf emirates like Dubai and Abu Dhabi is of course based on unique conditions—huge energy wealth and small populations—but it is also proof that modernity and Islam are not incompatible and that Arabs can make it in the ferociously competitive global age if they are willing to accept change and to project themselves positively into the future instead of being obsessed by the past.

The weight of memory and resentment constitutes the most severe obstacle to change. By investing massively in education, the Gulf emirates are opening the way of change, even as their mercantilist and consumerist passion restricts the meaning of hope.

For Latin America, change means above all transcending the

populist temptation and deepening the unification of the continent. It means leaving behind the negative definition of its identity. Latin America has the human and physical resources to become a continent of hope and opportunity. And the very same logic applies to Africa.

KNOWLEDGE IS THE ANSWER TO INTOLERANCE

Ignorance and intolerance go hand in hand. Peace and reconciliation are possible only among peoples who know and accept one another. In spite of the fact that we live in an information age, we do not understand the Other any better than we did in the past, in fact just the opposite: We are inundated by images and data that are obscuring rather than illuminating our vision of the world. Because the world we are living in is sure to grow more complex, cultures, nations, as well as individuals, will increasingly be obsessed with their identities. This obsession can only reinforce the weight of emotions in international politics.

But the interdependent, integrated world in which we live is simply too difficult to grasp and understand. It is a question of both quantity and quality: We humans have never been simultaneously so numerous, so diverse, and so varied in our lifestyles, values, and circumstances. It's tempting to try to escape such complexity by simply choosing to ignore it. Hence the appeal of fundamentalist religions and extreme ideologies, both of which reduce the world's complexity to the simplicity of slogans, catchphrases, and inflexible commands.

In such a world, emotions are reassuring. "I can no longer grasp or understand, let alone control, the world in which I live. Therefore I have to emphasize my differences with others and give priority to my emotions."

For this very reason, learning about the emotions of other cultures will become all the more crucial. The Other will increasingly become part of us in our multicultural societies. The emotional frontiers of the world have become as important as its geographic frontiers. And the two cannot be equated in a mechanical manner. With the process of time, the mapping of emotions will become as legitimate and compulsory an exercise as the mapping of geographical realities.

A cultural and historical grasp of the differences and similarities of the Other is the essential basis for a more tolerant world. For this reason, the teaching of history and culture should be made compulsory in any international relations study program. In their approach to the African continent, how many Western leaders are aware of its complex and rich precolonial history? How many are truly capable of shedding an unjustified sense of cultural superiority based on real and total ignorance? Africa has been for too long the most forgotten continent because it was and still largely is the most ignored and the least understood one. The same is true, if on a lesser scale, of our relations with Asia, Latin America, and even such "familiar" but complex foreign societies as that of Russia.

If knowledge and a minimal understanding of the Other are vital, so is self-knowledge. In fact the two are deeply intertwined, for only societies that are at ease with themselves can come to terms with others. Self-knowledge is particularly important in the case of Islam, where ignorance of one's own religion and culture constitutes the fertile soil for the most extremist interpretations, radical perversions, and the teaching of hatred. In this sense, the problem of Islam is our problem, and the culture of humiliation, though real, is exploited and exacerbated precisely by states and movements that are keen to use ignorance of Islam as a dangerous weapon of hatred. A selective process that cherry-picks the most intolerant formulas from the Koran is possible only because our knowledge of the world's sacred texts is so superficial.

WE NEED BOTH OPTIMISM AND A SENSE OF THE TRAGIC

My approach to history is based on a combination of deep optimism and the conviction that the world must and can be improved, if only at the margin, with a deep awareness of the tragic nature of historical processes. A realist in the world of idealists, I may also be seen as an idealist in the world of realists. How to reconcile ethics and geopolitics has been the main concern of my entire professional life.

The impulse that drove me to write about the geopolitics of emotion is at least in part based on personal history. As the son of a survivor of Auschwitz I was born with a deeply ingrained sense of tragedy. But the experience of my father, who survived the camps through a combination of luck, energy, hope, and the will to testify about what he went through, gave me something like a sense of mission. The central question my father's life posed to me, which I have been wrestling with for decades, is: Can the world we live in achieve even in part what my father achieved, the transcendence of fear and humiliation and the rekindling of hope, even in the face of tragedy?

This is an ambitious task, but hope and confidence are above all a state of mind. When Tristan Bernard, the Jewish French playwright, was about to be arrested in Nazi-occupied Paris, he said to his wife, "We had been living in fear, now we will live in hope."

To respond to the challenges we face, the world needs hope. This is, at bottom, the conviction and the message of this book.

ACKNOWLEDGMENTS

This book has not been a solitary exercise, but a true family adventure. My older son, Luca, has been not only my research assistant but a real intellectual and spiritual companion. I have greatly benefited from his philosophical culture, and he "held my hand" whenever I was seized by doubts. My wife, Diana Pinto, has read and reread my manuscript in its multiple versions. This book owes much to the depth of her commentaries and the strength of her deeply analytical and critical mind. As for my younger son, Laurent, he was based in Singapore at the time of my writing, and he has added his "Asian touch" to the manuscript.

My American editors, Charlie Conrad and Karl Weber, have played a major role in editing and adapting, if not tailoring, my Gallic way of thinking for an American and international audience. This book would simply not exist without them.

In the preparation for this book, I greatly benefited from friendly exchanges with many friends, colleagues, and students, in particular with Sergio Amaral, Jean-Claude Cousserand, Stanley Hoffmann, Roula Khalaf, Minxin Pei, Mahieddine Raoui, Olivier Roy, Shashi Taroor, and, last but not least, Martin Wolf.

This book, dedicated to emotions, owes much to the serene, green, and now peaceful surroundings in which it was mostly written—the Manche region of Normandy, the homeland of Alexis de Tocqueville as well as the site of some of the worst post-D-Day fighting of the Second World War more than sixty years ago. My months of writing there were made more delightful not only by the tranquil views of the countryside but also by the sound of Beethoven's music, which served as the accompaniment to my work, giving it hope and helping it to transcend the risks of fear and humiliation.

Notes

Preface

ix *Less than a month later:* "India Security Faulted as Survivors Tell of Terror," Yaroslav Trofimov et al., *Wall Street Journal*, December 1, 2008.

The Clash of Emotions

2 *Suketu Mehta, an Indian writer and journalist:* Suketu Mehta, "Mumbai, My Mumbai," *International Herald Tribune*, July 17, 2007.

4 *It was the passing of that era:* Francis Fukuyama, *The End of History and the Last Man* (New York: Free Press, 1992).

7 *Samuel Huntington's "clash of civilizations":* Samuel P. Huntington, *The Clash of Civilizations and the Remaking of World Order* (New York: Simon & Schuster, 1996).

7 *Pierre Hassner has opened my eyes:* Pierre Hassner, *Violence and Peace: From the Atomic Bomb to Ethnic Cleansing* (New York: Central European University Press, 1997).

7 *Stanley Hoffmann, the most open and generous teacher:* Stanley Hoffmann, *Duties Beyond Borders: On the Limits and Possibilities of Ethical International Politics* (Syracuse, N.Y.: Syracuse University Press, 1981). Also, Stanley Hoffman, Robert C. Johansen, and James P. Sterba, *The Ethics and Politics of Humanitarian Intervention* (Notre Dame, Ind.: University of Notre Dame Press, 1996).

1. *Globalization, Identity, and Emotions*

9 *Globalization may have made the world "flat"*: Thomas Friedman, *The World Is Flat: A Brief History of the Twenty-first Century* (New York: Farrar, Straus and Giroux, 2005).

9 *In his book The Lexus and the Olive Tree*: Thomas Friedman, *The Lexus and the Olive Tree* (New York: Farrar, Straus and Giroux, 1999), pp. 7–8.

10 *The French economist Daniel Cohen believes*: Daniel Cohen, *Three Lessons on Post-Industrial Society* (Cambridge, Mass.: MIT Press, 2008).

12 *The driving forces of globalization*: Martin Wolf, *Why Globalization Works* (New Haven, Conn.: Yale University Press, 2004).

16 *In sixteenth-century France the philosopher Jean Bodin*: Jean Bodin, *Les Six Livres de la République* (Paris: 1576).

2. *The Culture of Hope*

31 *Not for nothing is one of the best recent studies on India's miracle*: Edward Luce, *In Spite of the Gods: The Rise of Modern India* (Boston: Little, Brown, 2006).

34 *The Indian journalist and politician Jairam Ramesh*: Jairam Ramesh, *Making Sense of Chindia* (New Delhi: New Delhi Research Press, 2006).

35 *According to a recent Pew survey*: Pew Global Attitude Project, "China's Optimism: Prosperity Brings Satisfaction and Hope," November 16, 2005.

37 *"China is back" was the explicit message*: "China: The Three Emperors, 1662–1795." London: Exhibit at the Royal Academy of Arts, November 2005–April 2006.

39 *The demographic card is also being played*: Harry G. Gelber, *The Dragon and the Foreign Devils* (New York: Walker and Co., 2007), pp. 415–16.

40 *That reaction has accelerated "the return of Authoritarian Great Powers"*: Azar Gat, "The Return of Authoritarian Great Powers," *Foreign Affairs* (July–August 2007).

42 *In the words of Zbigniew Brzezinski*: Quoted in Gelber, op. cit., p. 418.

45 *The wealth of India was of a "spiritual nature"*: Amartya Sen, *The Argumentative Indian: Writings on Indian History, Culture and Identity* (New York: Picador, 2006), pp. xii–xiii.

47 *For example, as Edward Luce has noted*: Luce, op. cit., p. 221 ff.

48 *The rising confidence of upper-middle-class Indians*: Pavan K. Varma, *Being Indian: Inside the Real India* (London: Arrow Books, 2006), p. 186.

48 *A youthful nation (with 700 million out of 1.1 billion under the age of twenty-five)*: Luce, op. cit., p. 336.

50 *For the Dutch writer Ian Buruma*: Ian Buruma, *The Wages of Guilt: Memories of War in Germany and Japan* (New York: Vintage Books, 1995).

54 *One senior Western diplomat*: "Special Report on China," *Financial Times*, September 13, 2008.

3. The Culture of Humiliation

59 *According to a recent poll*: Amr Elbaz, "Hassan Nasrallah Tops Poll." Ahl-Alquran Web site, accessed October 13, 2008. Online at http://www.ahl-alquran.com/English/show_article.php?main_id=356.

61 *"We civilizations have learned we are mortal"*: Paul Valéry, "Réflections sur le Monde Actuel," 1922.

61 *It is as if the Arabs themselves*: Albert Hourani, *A History of the Arab Peoples* (London: Faber and Faber, 1991), p. 249.

61 *For the Egyptian economist Galal Amin*: Ibid., pp. 442–43.

62 *In the great Egyptian novel*: Alaa Al Aswany, *The Yacoubian Building* (New York: HarperPerennial, 2006). Adapted to film by Marwan Hamed, 2006.

62 *To quote Bernard Lewis*: "The 2007 Irving Kristol Lecture by Bernard Lewis," American Enterprise Institute Annual Dinner, March 7, 2007.

69 *For a Syrian philosopher quoted by Bernard Lewis*: Bernard Lewis, *Islam and the West* (New York: Oxford University Press, 1994), pp. 28–46.

69 *The United Nations' Arab Development Report*: United Nations, *Arab Human Development Report: Creating Opportunities for Future Generations* (New York: United Nations Publications, 2002).

69 *As the noted Middle East expert Olivier Roy has brilliantly demonstrated*: Olivier Roy, *Globalized Islam: The Search for a New Ummah* (New York: Columbia University Press, 2006).

70 *in the words of scholar James Piscatori*: "The Turmoil Within Islam," *Foreign Affairs*, May/June 2002.

70 *For Ali in her challenging essay*: Ayaan Hirsi Ali, *The Caged Virgin* (New York: Free Press, 2006).

73 *In a recently published book*: Mark LeVine, *Heavy Metal Islam: Rock, Resistance and the Struggle for the Soul of Islam* (New York: Three Rivers Press, 2008).

76 *Consider, as an example, the life and career:* Edward Said, Orientalism (New York: Vintage Books, 1978).

76 *In a recently released report:* New York Police Department (NYPD), "Radicalization in the Western World: The Domestic Threat," 2008. Excerpted in *Le Monde*, June 26, 2008.

78 *The Pakistani-born writer Mohsin Hamid has well expressed:* Mohsin Hamid, The Reluctant Fundamentalist (New York: Penguin Books, 2007).

80 *In "My Brother the Bomber," a fascinating study:* "My Brother the Bomber," *Prospect* (July 2005).

82 *Some intellectuals, like Jean Baudrillard in France:* Jean Baudrillard, The Spirit of Terrorism and Requiem for the Twin Towers (New York: Verso, 2002).

83 *Despite Philip Bobbitt's contention:* Philip Bobbitt, Terror and Consent: The Wars for the Twenty-first Century (New York: Alfred A. Knopf, 2008).

83–84 *Hossein Shariatmadari, the editor of the leading Persian newspaper:* "Influential Promoter of Islamic Revolution," *Financial Times*, September 28, 2007.

84 *In Being Arab, the last book he published:* Samir Kassir, Being Arab (New York: Verso, 2006).

87 *A recent sketch of life in Dubai:* Michael Slackman, "Young and Arab in Land of Mosques and Bars," *New York Times*, September 22, 2008.

4. The Culture of Fear

93 *"Fear misleads, sometimes quite seriously":* Peter N. Stearns, American Fear: The Causes and Consequences of High Anxiety (New York: Routledge, 2006), p. 201.

103 *In their excellent essay on France and its Muslims:* Jonathan Laurence and Justin Vaïsse, Integrating Islam: Political and Religious Challenges in Contemporary France (Washington, D.C.: Brookings Institution Press, 2006).

109 *This last question is of course a classic one:* Paul Kennedy, The Rise and Fall of the Great Powers (New York: Random House, 1987).

112 *In his very convincing book:* Philip Gordon, Winning the Right War: The Path to Security for America and the World (New York: Times Books, 2007); David Frum and Richard Perle, An End to Evil: How to Win the War on Terror (New York: Random House, 2004).

114 *In a recent column written from China:* David Brooks, "Harmony and the Dream," *New York Times*, August 11, 2008.

116 *The success of Fareed Zakaria's last essay:* Fareed Zakaria, The Post-American World (New York: W. W. Norton, 2008).

117 *Key politicians from both sides of the aisle:* Tamar Jacoby, "Immigration Nation," *Foreign Affairs* (November–December 2006).

121 *Some might answer this question:* Tony Smith, *A Pact with the Devil: Washington's Bid for World Supremacy and the Betrayal of the American Promise* (New York: Routledge, 2007).

122 *"Americans' faith in our values":* Anne-Marie Slaughter, *The Idea That Is America: Keeping Faith with Our Values in a Dangerous World* (New York: Basic Books, 2007).

5. Hard Cases

131 *If today some commentators who care for Africa:* Nicholas Kristof, "Africa: Land of Hope," *New York Times,* July 5, 2007.

133 *Aside from Rwanda, as Nicholas Kristof remarks:* Ibid.

133 *It is a continent between two worlds:* See Richard Dowden, *Africa: Altered States, Ordinary Miracles* (London: Portobello Books, 2008).

6. The World in 2025

154 *In Giuseppe di Lampedusa's celebrated novel:* Giuseppe Tomasi di Lampedusa, *Il Gattopardo,* 1958. Published in English as *The Leopard* (New York: Pantheon, 2007).

Selected Bibliography

Allen, Mark. *Arabs*. London: Continuum, 2006.

Appadurai, Arjun. *Fear of Small Numbers, An Essay on the Geography of Anger*. Durham and London: Duke University Press, 2006.

Ayalon, David. *Le phénomène mamelouk dans l'orient islamique*. Paris: PUF, 1996.

Barber, Benjamin R. *Jihad vs. McWorld: Terrorism's Challenge to Democracy*. New York: Ballantine Books, 2001.

Brzezinsky, Zbigniew. *Second Chance: Three Presidents and the Crisis of American Superpower*. New York: Basic Books, 2007.

Buruma, Ian. *Inventing Japan: From Empire to Economic Miracle*. London: Orion Books, 2005.

Buruma, Ian. and Margalit Avishai. *Occidentalism: The West in the Eyes of Its Enemies*. New York: Penguin Books, 2004.

Cooper, Robert. *The Breaking of Nations: Order and Chaos in the Twenty-first Century*. New York: Atlantic Monthly Press, 2003.

Dowden, Richard. *Africa: Altered States, Ordinary Miracles*. London: Portobello Books, 2008.

Drissi, Amar, and Thierry de Montbrial. *Dubai: The New Arab Dream*. Paris: IFRI, 2006.

Etzioni, Amitai. *From Empire to Community*. New York: Palgrave Macmillan, 2004.

Ferguson, Niall. *The War of the World: History's Age of Hatred.* London: Penguin Books, 2006.

Friedman, Thomas L. *The Lexus and the Olive Tree: Understanding Globalization.* New York: Farrar, Straus and Giroux, 1999.

—————. *The World Is Flat: A Brief History of the Twenty-first Century.* New York: Farrar, Straus and Giroux, 2005.

Gelber, Harry G. *Dragon and the Foreign Devils: China and the World, 1100 B.C. to the Present.* New York: Walker & Company, 2007.

Gordon, Philip H. *Winning the Right War: The Path to Security for America and the World.* New York: Times Books, 2007.

Habermas, Jürgen. *The Divided West.* Cambridge: Polity Press, 2006.

Hassner, Pierre. *La violence et la paix: De la bombe atomique au nettoyage ethnique.* Paris: Editions Esprit, 1995.

Hirsi, Ali Ayaan. *The Caged Virgin: A Muslim Woman's Cry for Reason.* London: Pocket Books, 2004.

Hoffmann, Stanley. *Duties Beyond Borders: On the Limits and Possibilities of Ethical International Politics.* Syracuse, N.Y.: Syracuse University Press, 1981.

Hopkins, A. G., ed. *Globalization in World History.* New York and London: W. W. Norton & Company, 2002.

Huntington, Samuel P. *The Clash of Civilizations and the Remaking of the World Order.* New York: Simon & Schuster, 1996.

—————. *Who Are We? America's Great Debate.* London: Simon & Schuster, 2004.

Husein, Ed. *The Islamist: Why I Joined Radical Islam in Britain, What I Saw Inside and Why I Left.* London: Penguin Books, 2007.

Hutton, Will. *The Writing on the Wall: China and the West in the 21st Century.* London: Little, Brown, 2007.

Kagan, Robert. *The Return of History and the End of Dreams.* New York: Alfred A. Knopf, 2008.

Kaplan, Robert D. *The Coming Anarchy: Shattering the Dreams of the Post Cold War.* New York: Vintage Books, 2001.

Kassir, Samir. *Being Arab.* London and New York: Verso, 2006.

Koch, Richard, and Chris Smith. *Suicide of the West.* London and New York: Continuum, 2006.

Kurlantzick, Joshua. *Charm Offensive: How China's Soft Power Is Transforming the World.* New Haven, Conn., and London: Yale University Press, 2007.

Laurence, Jonathan, and Justin Vaïsse. *Integrating Islam: Political and*

Religious Challenges in Contemporary France. Washington, D.C.: Brookings Institution Press, 2006.

Lewis, Bernard. *From Babel to Dragomans: Interpreting the Middle East*. London: Orion Books, 2005.

————. *The Middle East: A Brief History of the Last 2000 Years*. New York: Scribner, 1995.

Lovell, Julia. *The Great Wall: China Against the World, 1000 BC–AD 2000*. London: Atlantic Books, 2006.

Luce, Edward. *In Spite of the Gods: The Strange Rise of Modern India*. London: Little, Brown, 2006.

Mahbubani, Kishore. *Beyond the Age of Innocence: Rebuilding Trust Between America and the World*. New York: Public Affairs, 2005.

————. *The New Asian Hemisphere: The Irresistible Shift of Global Power to the East*. New York: Public Affairs, 2008.

Nafisi, Azar. *Reading Lolita in Tehran: A Memoir in Books*. New York: Random House, 2003.

Obama, Barack. *The Audacity of Hope: Thoughts on Reclaiming the American Dream*. New York: Canongate, 2006.

Pamuk, Orhan. *Istanbul: Memories of a City*. London: Faber and Faber, 2005.

Podhoretz, Norman. *World War IV: The Long Struggle Against Islamofascism*. New York: Doubleday, 2007.

Prestowitz, Clyde. *Rogue Nation: American Unilateralism and the Failure of Good Intentions*. New York: Basic Books, 2003.

Richardson, Louise. *What Terrorists Want: Understanding the Terrorist Threat*. London: John Murray, 2006.

Roy, Olivier. *Les illusions du 11 septembre: Le débat stratégique face au terrorisme*. Paris: La République des Idées, Seuil, 2002.

Said, Edward W. *Culture and Imperialism*. New York: Vintage Books, 1994.

————. *Out of Place, A Memoir*. London: Granta Books, 2000.

Sen, Amartya. *The Argumentative Indian: Writings on Indian History, Culture and Identity*. London: Allen Lane/Penguin Books, 2005.

Shlaim, Avi. *The Iron Wall: Israel and the Arab World*. London: Penguin Books, 2001.

Slaughter, Anne-Marie. *The Idea That Is America: Keeping Faith with Our Values in a Dangerous World*. New York: Basic Books, 2007.

Smith, Rupert. *The Utility of Force: The Art of War in the Modern World*. London: Penguin Books, 2006.

Smith, Tony. *A Pact with the Devil: Washington's Bid for World Supremacy and the Betrayal of the American Promise.* New York: Routledge, 2007.

Stearns, Peter N. *American Fear: The Causes and Consequences of High Anxiety.* London and New York: Routledge, 2006.

Tharoor, Shashi. *India: From Midnight to the Millennium.* New York: Arcade Publishing, 1997.

Trenin, Dmitri. *The End of Eurasia: Russia on the Border Between Geopolitics and Globalization.* Washington, D.C., and Moscow: Carnegie Endowment for International Peace, 2002.

Trofimov, Yaroslav. *The Siege of Mecca: The Forgotten Uprising in Islam's Holiest Shrine and the Birth of Al Qaeda.* New York: Doubleday, 2007.

Varma, Pavan K. *Being Indian: Inside the Real India.* London: Arrow Books, 2006.

Weapons of Mass Destruction Commission. *Weapons of Terror: Freeing the World of Nuclear, Biological and Chemical Arms,* 2006.

Wolf, Martin. *Why Globalization Works.* New Haven, Conn.: Yale University Press, 2004.

INDEX

ABOUT THE AUTHOR

Dominique Moïsi is a founder of the French Institute of International Relations (IFRI), where he is today a senior adviser. One of Europe's leading geostrategic thinkers, he is the first holder of the Pierre Keller Visiting Chair at Harvard University. A prolific author, he is a columnist for the *Financial Times* and writes a monthly column distributed by Project Syndicate.